EXPERT
—TO—
INFLUENCER

How to Position Yourself for
Meaningful Impact

DIVYA PAREKH

COPYRIGHT AND DISCLAIMER

ADVANCED PRAISE FOR EXPERT
TO INFLUENCER

I have the pleasure of interacting with Divya... Not only is Divya a caring influencer, but she's also about giving back too! Divya is fully dimensional, and when you decide to read this book about building genuine influence, you've made a great choice!

RHONDA VETERE
Global CIO/CTO, 2 Time author, Corporate Athlete and top 50 most powerful women in Technology in 2019
www.rhondavetere.com

Divya Parekh's book *Expert to Influencer* informs, guides, and ultimately inspires you to take ownership not just of your career but your life. It provides a provocative system that shows you how to become the best version of yourself, grow your influence while impacting masses. It is a must-read for entrepreneurs, leaders, and achievers!

STEVE HARRISON
Co-founder National Publicity Summit

Divya has been an influencer in my life, and she's done it again, sharing her inner secrets on impactful influence, where you can touch, move and inspire people's heart and bring transformation from within, the key to continuous growth and contribution.

KENNETH J. VAN LIEW, P.E.
International Bestselling Author, World-Renowned NYC Skyscraper Expert and Real Estate Development Authority

I have personally experienced Divya's amazing influence skills. In *Expert to Influencer*, Parekh tackles the subject of influence and impact – how people obtain it and what contributes to exceptional influence as opposed to everyday influence. If anyone could make the complicated journey of up-leveling yourself from an expert to an influencer easy and exciting, it's Divya. The book is absolutely a must-read for anyone curious in a much higher level of credibility, influence, and prosperity.

AMANDA MCDONOUGH
Movie and TV Actress, Author, and speaker
www.Amanda-McDonough.com

This book is a must-read for entrepreneurs, corporate leaders, authors, achievers... The book provides easy to follow step by step strategies and practical tactics to build influence and create an impact. Not only will it help you develop a genuine and compelling brand to inspire and impact your colleagues, friends, and audience, but also it will bring joy and fulfillment in your life.

MICHAEL GRECCO
World-famous celebrity photographer and TV personality

I have lived my life seeking to learn from the best, and my coaching experience with Divya has shown that Divya Parekh is one of the BEST in the world of influencers. This book is a benchmark system to ensure that experts exceed their potential. This book is a must-read if you want to unlock some of the closed doors of the business industry.

DR. MARY KAYE HOLMES,
#1 Bestselling Author

I heartily recommend this book to anyone managing a company or creating a new startup. Divya Parekh is a smart and experienced coach with clients around the world. Coach Divya has worked with corporate leaders, transforming them into high performers. She understands what the true power players do to achieve changes that others cannot. She has real-world experience and shares it generously with this new book."

JOHN MCKEE CEO
John McKee and Associates
www.JohnMcKeeandAssociates.com

Winners find a way to win. Losers tell themselves and everyone around them stories about why they lost and put the blame on everyone else for their failures. Every day, people all over the world are influenced by brands to make purchasing decisions, lifestyle choices, and much more. We spend trillions of dollars annually based upon how we are influenced by marketers, yet professionals mistakenly only sell their competence as a reason for being chosen. There are millions of experts and few influencers. Divya Parekh encourages you to step up and be big in her book, "Expert to Influencer," providing encouragement for you to stop hiding from being seen by the world and be seen for who you truly are.

JEFF ALTMAN
The Big Game Hunter
www.TheBigGameHunter.us

If you've dreamed of becoming an influencer in your field, this book is a must-read. Get ready to bust up the misconceptions, create a strategy that actually works, and enjoy the resources you need to succeed. The chapter on community building was a game-changer, and I can quickly see all the "secrets" I didn't have before. This is a brilliant, generous book that will catapult any entrepreneur into realizing their dreams much more quickly than they ever imagined."

LAURA DI FRANCO
Owner of Brave Healer Productions

"People have always found allegiance with people they trust," says Divya Parekh. To be honest, I hardly ever trust those who CALL themselves Influencers. I prefer to find those, who I can label this way. This book is about BECOMING one through values, actions, and brand. It is packed with self-discovery exercises that will help you create your own path. At the end of it you will not have to call yourself influencer. The others will do it for you.

INGA BIELINSKA
An executive coach and a business trainer
www.linkedin.com/in/ingabielinska

Leadership and influence are synonymous in that they both are reliant on one's actions inspiring another to say "yes" to the request. Divya has done an excellent job of breaking this down for readers to identify and develop their own ability to influence others with integrity.

PATRICK VERONEAU
MS. Podcast host of Lead Like No Other

Divya's love for connecting deeply and authentically with people truly comes out in this book. She patiently and methodically goes through, step-by-step, how to create a robust image and brand for yourself, which are values focused. Her chapters are chock-full with practical tips, thought-provoking questions which facilitate deeper reflection, and many examples and anecdotes that help clarify ideas. As I went through the book, I appreciated the balance between the high-level view and the tactical "how-to" that actually make things happen.

A great, simple yet robust guide to becoming an influencer…and very easy to read as well!

Rose Cartolari
Executive coach and former COO of Scharper,
a European pharmaceuticals company

If you want to boost your credibility and influence in the world, this book will help. I started my company over 30 years ago and now wish I had read this book back then. It would have helped me avoid countless mistakes. Even now, I am picking up some great ideas from it. Thank you, Divya, for sharing your insights and experience."

John J. Murphy
Award-winning author, speaker and business consultant

Divya Parekh's book: *Expert to Influencer* is a must read for those who want to understand the power of influence in life and career. She shares clear and actionable steps to hone your influence and live your authentic brand in an organization or in an entrepreneurial venture. In a noisy and overwhelming professional world, influencers rise above the fray to find meaning, purpose, and higher levels of passion and fulfillment in their careers.

CAROLINE DOWD-HIGGINS
Executive Coach, Speaker, Author, and Media Host
www.carolinedowdhiggins.com

Can you afford to be lost in the media crowd? Can you afford to be one more in a pile? Can you afford to be the best and nobody knows about it? I guess the answer is "NO." As entrepreneurs, branding yourself is the key to be seen or been missed. An information age classic. The brilliant and wise Divya Parekh shares her amazing breadth of experience and knowledge to unlock the roadmap of building massive influence. If you are ready to live up to your vision and take your message to masses, this is the one book and philosophy of predictable, unstoppable growth that you need to read!

SUSAN IBITZ
Human Behavior Hacker
www.Humanbehaviorlab.com

The reality is that for today's entrepreneur, "Passion Alone is Not Enough." To succeed in this highly competitive marketplace, small business professionals must accompany that passion with processes & procedures proven to work by other successful professionals. And, Divya Parekh's new book "Expert To Influencer" is full of real-world examples that produce real-world advice for every ambitious entrepreneur to follow. If you are ready to unpack your dreams with practical and simple to follow the process, step right this way, and get your copy today!

TR GARLAND
Award Winner, Speaker, Author, LinkedIn Expert

If you have an expertise in being a leader, an entrepreneur or a craftsman, and want to reach more people, this is the only roadmap you will need. If you want to make an impact, the kind that truly shifts the dial, **this is the only roadmap you will need.** It is the most practical, doable, and enjoyable guide I've ever read on obtaining influence. Divya is a beautiful storyteller who understands and relays from personal experience, just what to do, and what not to do on your journey from Expert to Influencer.

MICHELLE DOSS
*The CEO's Trusted Partner, Strategic Advisor,
and Executive Coach*

There isn't a person on the planet who wouldn't benefit from reading this book! Everyone, especially, entrepreneurs, need to read this book! As you know, entrepreneurship is not for the faint of heart. It takes an incredibly courageous and brave individual who is willing to confidently grow from within to create a thriving life and business. It takes more than just putting out a social media post from time to time and sending out an email here and there, but the question that still eludes so many is, "but, how do I actually do it?"

Look no further – this book is the missing piece of the puzzle which helps everyday corporate leaders, coaches, and other high achieving individuals to transform into becoming leading industry influencers.

Do yourself a favor and grab your own copy now!

LISA MARIE PEPE
Online Visibility Expert and The Confidence Coach
www.lisamariepepe.com

What kind of an
Influencer
are you?

Knowing your influencer type will help you understand your unique values, what are you most drawn to, and where your passions lie. Acting on this knowledge will help you realize more fulfillment in critical areas of your life and become more influential in creating the impact you want to!

https://success.divyaparekh.com/influencer-types

TABLE OF CONTENTS

Copyright And Disclaimer. II

Advanced Praise For Expert To Influencer. V

Dedication XIX

My Message To You – The Beginning Of Our Conversation . . . XXI

Introduction 1

Phase 1: Design It! **11**

   Chapter 1: What Is It? **13**

      Marketing 19

      Sales 19

      Positioning And Branding 20

      Positioning 21

      Branding 22

      Brand Experience. 23

      Brand Positioning 24

      The Process – Design It, Build It, Live It. 26

   Chapter 2: Who Is It For? **29**

      Design Phase. 31

      The Design Phase – Creating Clarity
      In Your Message 33

      Who Are You? 33

      Establish Your Values. 34

      Activity – Values Assessment. 34

      Swot Analysis. 37

      Passions. 39

      Who's Your Market? 40

      Segment Your Market 40

      Brand Connection 44

      Branding Misconceptions 46

Chapter 3: Why Is It Important? **53**

Why It's Important To Your Audience 55

Why Is Branding Important?. 57

Why Is Influencing Important? 60

Defining How You Want To Be Seen 63

Why It's Important To Invest In Your Brand 64

If You Don't, They Will 65

Activity - Positive And Negative Influencers. 67

Chapter 4: Where Do They Get It? **71**

Phase 2: Build It! **81**

Chapter 5: How Do You Do It?. **83**

Build Phase. 85

Crafting Your Personalized, Definitive Marketing
Message To Create Your Standout Brand 87

Make Your Message A Movement 89

Your Persona 91

Your Tagline 93

Brand Promise 95

The Standout Test 96

Chapter 6: How Do You Deliver It? **101**

Powerful Marketing And Sales Platform. 103

Choosing Your Platform Type 106

Building Your Platform. 109

Content. 110

Persuasion 113

Repurposing Content. 117

Keep The Fire Burning. 118

Social Media 119

Keywords. 121

To Write A Book Or Not? 122

Chapter 7: How Do You Scale It? **127**

    Influencer Growth Strategy 129

    Grow Your Brand Community. 129

    Grow Your Peer Community. 132

    Grow Your Influencer Community. 133

    Creating Partnerships 138

Phase 3: Live It!. **141**

Chapter 8: How Do You Live It? **143**

    Live Your Brand Phase 144

    An Authenticity Byte. 144

    Transparency 145

    Giving 146

    Giving Back To Your Community 147

    Grow Internal Relationships 148

    Connect With Your Community. 148

    How To Give Back. 149

    When Something Goes Wrong 150

    When You Get Off Track 152

Chapter 9: How Does All This Work For A Corporate Leader? **155**

    Corporate Businesses And Professionals 156

    Personal Branding 157

    CEO 159

    Positional Leaders (C-Suites, VPs, Directors, Managers, And Supervisors) 161

    Corporate Professionals 165

Chapter 10: How Does All This Work For An Entrepreneur? **171**

    Entrepreneurs. 172

    Building Trust Online 173

    Relationship Building 174

Influencer Marketing. 175
Instagram. 177
Security. 178
What's Next 181
Acknowledgments 183
About Divya 187
Index 189

DEDICATION

To you, who recognizes the calling of heart,

Ruminate you might, yet you yearn to start fresh

To you, who wants to finish what you start

Leave the past, it's time to thresh

You know when you know

It's a feeling! It's energy

Without the rain there is no rainbow

Together, there is a synergy

To you, who is ready to feel alive

Infuse nature with nurture

Together, let's strive to thrive

To you, my hope for the future

To you, who is a groundbreaker

You see what I see in you

A courage filled influencer

Light your purpose and passion anew

Let's ride the wave!

Here's to your new success!

Divya

MY MESSAGE TO YOU – THE BEGINNING OF OUR CONVERSATION

Since childhood, experiencing the beach and the vast ocean is one of my life magnets. Every time I visit, I bring back the ocean's essence with me in my heart as well as in videos I take to incorporate into my meditation practice. For a moment, picture yourself walking on the beach, and then playing in the waves. Feel the surge of the wave as you're lifted by its undulating power. Now, imagine a similarly savoring life, whether you are experiencing waves of a quality lifestyle, financial freedom, and impacting people all over the world. Feel the joy coursing through your blood as you experience the ripple effect of your influence!

The draw of the sea has beckoned humanity from the dawn of human society. When you see the ocean, the movement of waves is expected. WATER DOES NOT TRAVEL IN WAVES. Water does not transmit energy, WAVES DO! Waves have the potential to travel vast expanses of ocean, leaving each molecule of water behind for the next wave that comes along. The wind is the instigator of waves as it blows across a body of water.

Similarly, there is an age-old longing in humans to connect with purpose and make an impact. This hunger eclipses many other desires humans have. I was no stranger to this aspiration. During coaching, mentoring, and teaching in academia, in the corporate world as biopharmaceutical, and in the online world, as I became an entrepreneur, I have had the privilege of serving thousands of people across six continents in their quests to connect and realize dreams.

My enormous love of people, my fierce passion for serving others to help them succeed, my commitment to building leaders, and my unbridled desire to create a better world have given me the courage to be perfectly imperfect and help others do the same, all while deeply connecting with my fellow humans.

I experience fear, like any other human being. As with any new undertaking, I am experiencing it as I sit here today writing this message. Even talking to you on paper is a little scary. We may face a few wipeouts on the journey, but surface and go for it again and again. It is to answer the calling because you desire that incredible feeling of success. Like when a new surfer finally hops up on the board without falling and feels the power of the wave lifting them, taking them towards the sandy beach. It is, indeed, exhilarating! The payout is worth enduring the fear.

One of the hardest things a person can do is to become self-aware of who he or she is. It is also the most productive. Once we are honest with ourselves about our strengths, our weaknesses, and what we want in life, we can be unstoppable in fulfilling our dreams and goals. Such introspection is not easy for everyone. However, that journey to discover our true self will open unlimited doors for an individual. The fear of digging deep can be real, but know that on the other side, you will ride that wave of exhilaration!

There's the aspiration, and then there is actuality. For many people, the two do not align. However, with the right focus and a dash of gumption, they can be aligned, and should be! That's why I wrote this book. How does this all tie in with setting out to be an influencer in whatever you choose? Let's look at the connections.

There is a school of thought that it takes three steps to achieve full awareness of who you are. Each step takes time, so it isn't as quick as you might think to get to the end of this road. The first step is becoming aware of your body; not only while you are sitting there reading this, but in everything you do – walking, running, diving into the ocean, hugging a child, feeling the aches of lost loved ones, or some other woe. You get the picture. The practice of observation trains your brain to be aware of everything that you do. It is essential to understand this because understanding your mind is the next step. You want to comprehend how your analytical skills work, how your imagination clicks, and what your thoughts are, as well as to understand how you think. The final piece of the puzzle is to have a handle on your emotions – what triggers them, which ones rule your life, and how they affect your body and mind. As your awareness of emotions increases, your heart deepens, and the wind of consciousness heightens your energy to create transformational waves.

If you are a leader in a business or an organization or aspiring to such a role, you are aware that what I summarized is a process. Whatever we do for a living involves a progression of activities. Even an artist has a method to produce what they see in their mind and feel in their heart. As you see above, doing something like figuring out who you are is a process. When you approach any task – even self-awareness – with mindfulness and discipline, you are going to see positive results by the effort.

Together, we will go through systematic steps to go from expert to authority to influencer. This process is about using your substance and expertise and whatever style you decide to use to get your message out to the masses. It is about harnessing the energy to create your wave of influence.

As you confidently share your expertise with others, whether it is through your book or speaking or blogging or leading, and as others begin to respond and follow you, you step into a position of authority. It is when you are in that small percentage of experts whose voice makes a difference that people start to see you elevating above other experts. Achieving this recognition might happen in small ways like at conferences or responding to your posts on social media, but you become more and more recognized for what you know.

It is when you scale this authority that you leap into that exciting, and maybe scary, realm of influencer. It is where thousands listen to you and follow your lead and perhaps become influencers themselves. Your power radiates to many levels as your influence grows.

However, to quote a "*Spiderman*" movie, "With great power comes great responsibility." So let's dive into this new world of influencing as we bring our hearts, minds, and conviction to do what is right into the fold.

This book has one purpose: to acknowledge the influencer you are and help you connect with your inner potential with an understanding that your life will never be the same again. I hope that your aspiration of manifesting your potential will become unstoppable because this is your choice, your prerogative, your destiny!

"It's your turn! Now, is the time to know yourself and the people you serve. Consistently deliver this profound knowledge to connect and uplift humanity, and others will follow to become impactful influencers along with you."

– Divya Parekh

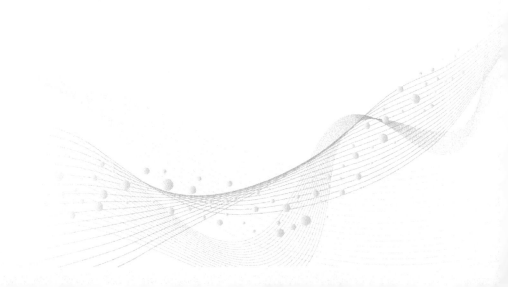

INTRODUCTION

*O*ur robot broke down... several times. Other robots had beaten it severely. It fought valiantly but finally gave up in the end. It was a trooper, hanging in there until the last minute. Our students had been using 3D printed parts which kept breaking down. They didn't have the big funding budgets other teams had so they needed to be innovative and mentally strong to work with what they had on hand. I started mentoring these students three years ago, and I have pulled back a little more each year so that they could take the lead. Last year, the student leaders stepped up with barely any input from me as their business leadership mentor.

We continued to work through the season gallantly. The team had poor results in the first regional competition receiving no awards, but their spirits stayed high. They were cheering each other on as they cheered other teams. Then we got to the second regional competition at Asheville. It was another event that did not go as the kids hoped, but they continued to fight. The judges stopped by their pit several times to question various members of the team.

As the team awards got announced after the competition ended, we knew that we would not receive one. However, the judges announced that they were going to give one additional award for emotional intelligence and leadership. They were awarding this team because they had kept their cool despite many setbacks. Imagine my reaction when they named our team! As the music blasted throughout the stadium, I sat in my seat and did not run down with them as they did high fives with the judges. I was soaking up the moment and feeling the ripple effect that started several years ago with these students. In three short years, the student leaders were making a difference for themselves and their team, and it got recognized.

The short story above happened to me recently. Besides being incredibly proud of the robotics team I mentor, I believe this is an excellent example of the power we can have as an influencer. While it is not strictly in my field of working with entrepreneurs and corporate leaders, helping young people is one of my passions. I know I had a positive influence on this team over my time with them, and I know my example and suggestions contributed to their recognition at this competition. That is what an influencer does. He or she shares their knowledge, ideas, and motivation so that the audience or community they have assembled can further spread their words and information.

I am here to partner with you to become an influencer, and I'm thrilled you opened this book. You might only be planning to check out the introduction and skim a few pages, but I am inviting you in so that we can connect and have a meaningful conversation for a while. Get a cup of coffee or your favorite beverage and listen to how you can become an influencer in your profession or industry. My community considers me such an influencer, and I am grateful for that. One of my objectives in my profession is to help others realize their potential to become influencers in their own right. I won't pull any punches with you. The truth is that you may take some wrong turns that appeared to be a good idea at the time and experience a failure or two. However, I am with you every step of the way, cheering you on and sharing my experiences as well as those of others as they traveled their journeys to achieve a meaningful impact. You have the advantage of avoiding our mistakes and learning the concepts that work well.

Influencers are born, not made. You can pick them out on the playground in an instant. It's the kid telling everyone else what game they will play next and how he or she is going to organize it. All the other kids immediately line up to get started.

It's also the young girl offering solace and companionship to her classmate who's feeling blue. The other girls follow her lead and join in with their empathy and support. The funny thing is that some of those other girls knew what they should do, but it wasn't natural for them to go over to the classmate and put their arms around her. Once the influencer did so, then whatever inhibitions the other girls had vanished.

During the teen years, high school influencers overtly choose who's in the group and who is not. Then they subtly decide where their group meets up in the morning before school starts, and where they eat lunch every day, and who gets invited to the party. Things aren't so different in college. Think back on those years in your education. Did the pictures I painted have you automatically pulling names and faces up from your memory, and were you labeling them, "Influencer"?

Fast forward to your first professional position where most people are a bit wet behind the ears in crafting their career. At this stage of your work life, hardly anyone is in a top influencer role. Even then, you can pick out those who have influencer in their DNA even if they aren't propped up with leadership titles or roles. They are the ones that attract opportunities in the workplace others do not get. They find solutions to problems that others can't see, and they have a following of people who are magnetically attracted to them. They are usually extraordinarily positive, and voraciously energetic, leaving behind the pessimists and passion-killers for growth and opportunity.

What do they look like in their prime? Influencers are in the spotlight. They are well-known in their circles, and people look up to them, hoping to learn from their success to create a life they want to live. Opportunities seek out the influencers, or they create them with ease and success. They have magnanimous personalities and find endless ways to attract more people into their tribe. Their passion and energy are extreme and infectious. They are helping others, and they have the drive to do it. How did they get there?

Rome wasn't built in a day, nor are top influencers. While influencers may be born with the genetic predisposition to lead, they fortify their behaviors over the years as each opportunity to lead others validates the previous actions, and over time everything they believe, think, and do is synonymous with their personal branding as an influencer.

Influencers are at home in the spotlight, and they never shy away from who they are. The authenticity that radiates naturally from top influencers comes because it stems from deep within. Their intrinsic motivation was created at conception and cultivated each step along the way.

When I have shared this insight with others, I often hear, "Great! Influencers are born. I might as well stop imagining myself as one of them."

That is where you are wrong. I believe everyone has an inborn influencer. Unlike the kid who runs the playground or the leader of the "cool" group in school, being an influencer doesn't always manifest itself early. For some, it can take a specific event where the scales fall off the eyes, and a person says, "I can do that!" Others have to be coaxed and taught how to get their inner influencer to come out and shine to the world. It comes down to recognizing that you have internal knowledge that you are an influencer. You understand your unexpressed potential. There have been signs all along the way, but you haven't had the right roadmap to lead you to the top. Here you are, learning and growing and figuring it all out. Be proud of yourself for undertaking the journey.

You know this. Whether it lies right below the surface in you or is deep within your soul, you are thirsting to follow the direction of creating significance in your life. Rather than trying to create something from the unknown, or to be somebody you're not, influencers learn how to extend their genuine self out to attract people and build a community around their values and ideals. The number one rule of becoming an influencer is to be true to yourself. That is the only way a person can sustain the impact over a long period.

INTRODUCTION

There is no discrimination when it comes to discovering your influencer soul. Your age does not matter; neither does being an introvert. It doesn't care if fear holds you tight within its grip, or if you think that others have already said everything worth telling. Your influencer soul trumps overwhelming odds, doubts, uncertainties, and limiting beliefs. Your influencer soul believes the time is now to declare to yourself and others, "I am ready to step into my vision and give myself the permission to release the genius I have within me; I am all in and I am going to create my future starting today."

It also doesn't matter if you are a CEO or an entrepreneur, a small business owner or a corporate professional. The call is there, and you are ready to be an influencer. Some people may have held that title from the time they woke up for that first day of pre-school. However, most of us have to dig down a bit further to bring it out of ourselves. Let's get to it; it's time you took the stage.

As a recovering corporate professional, and now an influence building strategic advisor, I have often checked in and asked, "What is the purpose of my life?" In the here and now I ask, "Why am I even writing this book?"

The answer to both questions is that I delight in experiencing the deep human connectivity that comes from helping others achieve their purpose and success in life, and I am particularly drawn to work with people who are ready to step onto the stage and own it. I love the joie de vivre that influencers have. As influencers, we trade our extreme levels of energy to boost us to even higher levels of passion and fulfillment. When two influencers are riding their dragons at the same time and at full speed, look out, world! Don't get in our way because we've got stuff to do!

As with any craft, processes and systems help elevate and accelerate the path to becoming an influencer. Studying and researching influencer territory is my passion and life. My goal is to bring you my experiences and learnings including the good and the bad. My hope for you is that you become an impactful influencer, and I promise to share as much as I can in these pages. Please understand that I can't possibly fit everything I know about influence in one book. If you ever want or need more information, support, or to accelerate your journey even faster, I am only an email away. (contact@divyaparekh.com)

Together we are going to elevate and hasten your path to becoming an influencer. That's why you bought the book, and it's why I wrote it. Our agreement is that from cover to cover, we are in this together. If you let your heart, mind, and spirit move forward in sync with the book, you will find yourself in a very different place when you close the back cover of this book. I am delighted for you, and especially for your followers. Because in the end, it is all about them, isn't it? As you experience success and deliver an impact on your community, I would love to share your accomplishments and impact with my thousands of followers.

Here's a brief preview of what we are embarking on together. Influencers know how to brand themselves, they know how to position that brand, and they know more about their target audience than the audience knows about themselves. We are going to do a deep dive into the world of marketing, but not for the reason you might think. Top marketers know that the psychology of emotions is the foundation of influence. It's not just what you say (your message), or how you say it (your delivery), it's how you create your message based on who you are and who your audience is. It's how you package your message into a brand, and how you position your brand to attract people. It's also how you deliver your brand through your platform, so more and more people can find you. Finally, it comes down to how you show up every day, to be the living and breathing manifestation of your authentic influencer brand. It is about the impact you create and how far reaching it is.

If we want to make a difference, it is important to touch people's hearts and bring the change from inside out. The key is in continuous learning, growth, and improvement. It is important to view yourself as an influencer because you can make a difference. Once you change your line of thinking, you can change your behavior. Between the trigger and the reaction lies the power of choice. The power of a right decision makes you create changes to reach unparalleled heights, expand your life in unimagined dimensions, and create a meaningful impact.

It is not that we do not want to make a difference, but sometimes, we don't know how. Influence is not merely inspiring others by words, but it is a combination of several strategies and skill sets. By learning and practicing them, you can impact people through your words, actions, and behaviors. The key is to create a strategy that resonates with your people and draws them into your community or tribe. As you continue to master your craft, you learn to focus on strategies that matter to gain multiplicity in reaching out to others.

This multiplicity expands your message, your impact, and the number of new followers you bring to your group. What results is real power because you touch people's hearts and that makes an impact. The key is to unlock the goodness from within and share with others such that it multiplies and increases tenfold. That is the beauty of being an influencer. When done nobly and gallantly and based on a love of humankind, an influencer can reach many people through their efforts.

Take a look at these people: Andrew Carnegie, Melissa Gates, Desmond Tutu, Nelson Mandela, Mother Theresa, Richard Branson, and Princess Diana. These are people from different nations, backgrounds, and callings in life. In different ways, they all became influencers who had a profound effect on their followers and the world. Their beliefs and goals were magnified and carried forward by their followers to make an impact they might never have thought was possible.

When mutual caring and respect are in place with a shared goal for the greater good, the future takes a turn towards uncharted territories that transcends the daily humdrum into a realization of inner potential. When you are responsible for others' successes, then you step into the role of an influencer. As you grow your influence, people perceive your community and you as one. You become an extension of your community, and your community is an extension of you because you are working together to achieve the outcomes that you care about. It requires resilience, a desire to make a difference, and the mastery of your craft.

Let's get back to that "meaning of life" concept. What is the overarching purpose of your life? What is the legacy you want to leave behind and live every single day you have left? Does the way you show up align with your purpose? How do you see yourself? How do others perceive you? Are they the same?

We'll get into all of this in detail later, but for now, take a moment to pause and answer each of those questions, one by one. They are not rhetorical; they are essential foundational questions for the journey ahead. Do not hurry the work we will do here. Each step requires deep internal and external reflection. If I may, I offer this one piece of advice – do not rush the process. Trust it, do the work, and you will reap what you sow.

Your meaning is directly related to what kind of influencer you are becoming. You have expertise in your craft and continuously seek to further your mastery. You are an expert in what you do. You may even be an authority on the subject, meaning you know more about it than many of the experts. How do we transfer this expertise, this authority, this vast amount of knowledge to the masses that most need it?

We move from being an expert or authority to becoming an influencer. It's no longer enough for us to have this knowledge; it is paramount that we share it with those that genuinely need it. Every day you hold onto this knowledge, there are people out there wishing they knew what you know. It's on us to give them what they need.

It is time to step into the spotlight and make a difference. Lead with love, courage, and authenticity. Inspire others to follow suit. Bring your giving heart to the equation with sincerity of helping others to succeed. As we work our way into a deeper understanding of influence, the combination of sharing your expertise and your genuine desire to make an impact will be your guiding light on the journey.

Make no mistake; becoming an influencer is a journey. There will be stops on the way where you are happy where you are, but the odds are good that you will want to expand your influence on even more people in the future. You will want to expand your reach from primary to secondary to tertiary and beyond. That is what drives change! Most Influencers find that the journey never ends as there are always ways to improve or a need to keep up on current trends to remain relevant. Following this book will be your GPS to establishing a firm foundation for your journey.

Before we jump in, I have a few helpful suggestions for you. I will be sharing several activities throughout this book. Whether your preference for note taking is on paper or computer, know that I will be inviting you to write and sketch, hence, choose your note-taking tool accordingly. Create an influencer journal that you can dedicate for this work. Remember, the more actively you engage in the activities, the more you will learn, and the more successful will be the impact you create.

With structure comes freedom!

PHASE 1

DESIGN IT!

"A brand is a message with the responsibility of making and delivering the promise to your tribe because you are going to inspire, influence and impact them. Their well-being is at the core of the brand. When that happens, positioning is easy."

– Divya Parekh

CHAPTER 1

WHAT IS IT?

*A*manda looked gloomily out the window of the small suite of offices she leased three months ago. For her, moving here from working out of her dining room was a highlight of her fledgling business. While working at a corporate consulting organization that focused on helping companies improve their leadership, management, and organization components, Amanda made an important observation. Many of these companies were not only lacking in providing training in the areas her company was excellent in, but they didn't do an outstanding job in software and IT training either. When she approached her boss about this, she explained to Amanda that the company had tried to provide those skills in the past, but it took away the focus of delivering. So, the technical training was phased out after a year.

For the next several months, Amanda continued to observe the companies she worked with and saw it was an ongoing issue in many companies and organizations. She had been thinking for a while about starting her own consulting business, but she initially thought it would be along the same lines as the company that employed her. After spending a month assembling data and a tentative organizational plan, she approached her boss with what she wanted to do. Amanda received her boss' blessing as well as an understanding they would complement each other as they worked with clients. Her new company would let her old one know when a company needed leadership and management training, and her old company would tell Amanda when software and IT expertise was required.

Amanda's first hire was Steve, a friend from college who knew more about computers, software, internet, and everything else connected with them than anyone Amanda knew. Steve was an IT specialist and was with a company who under-utilized him. He leaped at the chance to try something new. In the beginning, things worked well for her new company, IT Training Specialists. She quickly secured some contracts from her old contacts in companies she visited in her role with her former company. She recruited and hired a few trainers, and Steve supervised and trained them. The business snowballed and, after six months, Amanda leased the office space and ran her operations from there.

Now, three months later, Amanda felt like her company was in a rut. They were still getting new clients, but not at the rate they did in the beginning. She expected to have hired at least a dozen more people by now, but she held off. Because acquiring new business had tapered off, her current staff could handle things fine. Amanda wondered how to get off the plateau she felt the company was stuck on.

Steve came into her office and sat down. Looking at her, he said, "Stop worrying. Things will pick up."

Amanda turned from the window and put her hands on a folder. "You know that definition of insanity, the one that Einstein says that 'Insanity is doing the same thing over and over and expecting a different result?'"

Steve laughed and said, "Sometimes I feel like I'm living it every day."

"I think I am going to do something different," said Amanda. "I have been looking at some material in here," she continued as she tapped the folder.

"What's in the folder?" asked Steve.

Opening it, she said, "When I started this enterprise, I hired you to take care of the technical side – train the trainers, plot a curriculum for each client and deliver. I was going to run the business side and meet new clients, run HR, marketing, and whatever else we needed. Our evaluations are excellent from our clients, but we need to ramp up. I am not sure how, so I decided to look for help on the business side. I talked to a woman – her name is Mia – who helps people make their companies more prominent. She has a good track record. The owners of some of those companies that she helped become successful go out and talk to others about how to make their business prosper. She calls them influencers."

"You want to be an influencer?" asked Steve.

"No, I only want us to grow like I know we can."

"I suppose it can't hurt to give it a try," said Steve. "We can always use more ideas." He stood up. "I came in to tell you that I am heading over to Apex Manufacturing. I am meeting their IT guy to finalize the program we are going to do with them. He is a nervous Nellie type. He said his boss wants to be a success, and that is all that matters. Even if he takes down half the staff while doing it."

"Have fun," said Amanda. "Remind me never to get that way. As it is, I want to do something good with some of our profits as soon as we get a little more growth and consistency."

As Steve left, Amanda thought about what he said. She thought, "Success isn't a bad thing. It's what we all want. I guess it depends on how you get it." The word "success" kept nagging at her brain. One thing Amanda got out of her first meeting with Mia was that the name of her company was not exceptional. As she leaned back and closed her eyes, she wondered if she could use the word "success" somewhere in the name. Hmmm. She'd have to think about that one. She wanted others to notice her company!

*   *   *

As you continue reading this book, you are going to see the evolution and success of Amanda and Steve's business venture. We are not only going to talk about theory here; we will see how to apply it.

To understand how I share my work as an influencer, it will be helpful to you to know how I define several terms.

Let's start with "influence." Influence is the way a person impacts others without force. It's messaging, heart to heart, and it is a widespread net. It changes others for the better, and in doing so, changes the world.

I am also going to be using specific terms and definitions for marketing, sales, and other facets of running a company or an organization. For the most part, I will define them from the perspective of the seller and not the buyer. If you are focused on your personal brand instead of a business brand, each of these concepts apply as well. All you have to do is substitute "person" for "business."

Let's begin with a review of the most successful brands and what makes them thrive. Pick any of the top brands in the world to review their history of marketing, branding, and positioning, and you will see how they move from people considering them an expert to authority, and, finally, to that penultimate place in the market – influencer. Forbes' List of the World's Most Valuable Brands names include Apple, Google, Microsoft, Facebook, and Amazon as the top five. As darlings of the twenty-first century, they capitalized on technology and experience to win our hearts and minds. Some of the older companies are still holding steady in the top ten by consistently delivering products and experiences – Coca-Cola, Samsung, Disney, Toyota, and McDonald's. Even Starbucks at #34 figured out how to sell a 50¢ cup of coffee for $4.00 by providing a unique and innovative experience.

The commonality in the marketing for all these brands is the experience. People want more than a good product or service. They want to feel good when they invest their time and money, and these examples of the top brands in today's marketplace validate the concept that experience wins. The key to defining what kind of experience your market wants is to understand who they are, give them what they need, and then make them feel good about it.

Oprah certainly was not considered an expert when she landed her first TV job as a part-time co-anchor on the local evening news at WVOL. However, with her vision, she brought talk shows into the entertainment mainstream. Because the talk show medium provided a more intimate communication platform, Oprah was not only winning over many female (and male) viewers but also, she revolutionized social conversations by creating an entry point for LGBT people in media. She spoke openly about her abusive past and gave a voice to an entire generation of people who had previously been silenced by convention. After redefining her focus to literature, self-improvement, and spirituality, she left the talk-show circuit and created her TV channel. Quite a few have criticized her for creating an emotion-centric environment that promotes confessional culture and conversations around controversial topics. Oprah's endorsement of President Obama for the presidential nomination in 2007 emerged as a solid political force that may have helped Obama win the race. Whether you like her or dislike her, Oprah is an icon. She's won too many awards to list and was named one of the top five richest self-made women in the world for multiple years.

I chose to use Oprah's story because it clearly shows the maturation of her as a person, and moreover, of her brand. Check out Wikipedia and read through her entire history (so far), and you'll see how many times she has rebranded/repositioned who she is and how she wants the world to see her. Over the years, Oprah continually made strategic decisions to define her focus and narrow her target market. As she stands true to them, she massively grows her influence.

Recently the #27 brand on the list, IKEA, announced they were opening a new location in Cary, NC. The excitement was crazy and unexpected by this former NYC college student. I didn't think IKEA's brand was a good match for the people in Cary, a close suburb to the Research Triangle Park and home to the highest concentration of PhDs in the country. It is an established, family-oriented town. I wasn't surprised when they pulled the plug stating the area did not fit their target market of urban chic. This dedication to their brand and understanding their market permitted them to back out once they researched the area. Making strategic decisions to narrow your target market and then standing true to that market is a cornerstone of branding success.

Whether you are CEO of a business or CEO of yourself, how others perceive you is all too important. Unless we have a definitive "marketing strategy," opinions are left to chance and are often vastly misconstrued from what we desire or believe. Thus, it behooves us to spend some time developing how we want others to see us. By putting these strategies into motion and staying true to them over time, people's perception of your brand will match with the message you want to share with them.

One of the biggest challenges in designing your marketing strategy is to understand the array of marketing concepts out there. It's no surprise that marketing and sales terms are confusing, with so many creative people having a hand in defining them over the years. Know that you may find other ways to define these terms. However, I will define them with perspective to the information I am sharing in this book. Then we'll get down to the fun stuff!

MARKETING

Marketing is one of the primary strategies of a business. It is an ongoing communications exchange with prospects, customers, and those we want to influence so we can teach, inform, and build relationships over time. It includes research, positioning and branding, market perceptions, communicating, targeting, advertising, public relations, market analysis, and everything you do to reach and influence your prospects and customers. This process is how you get others to buy what you are selling or delivering.

SALES

Sales is an exchange of a commodity for money, and includes interpersonal interaction, engagement, pitching an offer, negotiating price, and finalizing a deal. You may be selling a product, a service, or an idea.

In comparison, marketing is to sales as plowing is to planting for a farmer. Marketing builds goodwill with your audience so that you can pitch your product or service or cause to them. For now, we'll leave sales to another book.

There are a few additional marketing terms I'd like to point out since they are often part of a marketing strategy.

Public Relations is nurturing and sustaining trust in the relationship between a company, organization, or an individual with the market or customer or prospective customer. We use public relations to keep your brand in front of your audience in order for them to get to know you, like you, and remember how great you are!

Advertising involves two phases. Individuals, organizations, and associations pay to connect with their target audience. The first phase consists of identifying relevant mediums to promote an individual, an organization, a service, a product, or a cause. The second phase involves creating an advertisement or ads that will resonate with the target audience in a way that makes people support an individual or an organization or a cause or purchase the service or product advertised. Advertising focuses on communicating a message to your target audience using mostly paid media. Successful advertising programs include foci that link company mission, branding, and services, as well as specific product information.

POSITIONING AND BRANDING

As with overall marketing strategy, Positioning and Branding also apply to both businesses and people. In this book, we will explore positioning and branding for corporate and entrepreneurial businesses, as well as personal positioning and branding for CEOs, corporate professionals, and entrepreneurs. As different as these perspectives may be, many tenets are fundamental to all. To distinguish between positioning and branding, I'll share the following definitions and examples. Branding and positioning are closely related, yet they're very different in detail.

POSITIONING

Positioning is much what you would expect it to be about. It is how your customers rank you in relation to the other industry players. Positioning emerges from differentiating yourself from the other market leaders. In other words, what do you offer or do differently from all the other businesses that provide the same products or services? As with branding, we can passively land in a particular position in the market. Ideally, we identify where we want to target the market and develop a specific strategy to ensure we achieve that desired position.

Positioning provides a unique distinction and advantage to your brand to build trust with your target market and establish your brand as a caring partner. After choosing a specific target market area, companies will research those markets to determine who the key players are, and then they will study the players to understand their products and services, relationship with their target market, marketing methodology, pricing, reputation, delivery guarantees, distribution channels and more. After researching, the company determines how to carve out a unique position based on its attributes. Once a company positions itself for success, it can then strengthen its brand identity by claiming that position within the marketplace.

To understand how to position successfully, you must know your competition intimately and understand their unique competitive difference from all others in the same market. Entire careers concentrate on market intelligence, and large companies spend millions trying to keep abreast of the dynamic positioning of others in their market.

Consider how Chipotle entered the Mexican fast food market. Chipotle is a fast-casual restaurant chain dedicated to using responsibly raised food in its burritos, burrito bowls, salads, and tacos. The brand's founder, Steve Ells, originally wanted to create a new fast food experience focused on great tasting food made with high-quality ingredients. As he learned more about his market and what people wanted, he focused on how to morph people's thinking not only about fast food but also eating habits. Due to food safety issues in their supply, their branding message of commitment to "food with integrity" was sidetracked in 2016. However, the company recovered financially and remains one of the top brands for their purposely defined sub-market. By positioning itself as a fast food chain that delivers healthy food, they carved out a section of the fast food market that genuinely cares about eating food that is responsibly and sustainably grown, distributed, and served.

BRANDING

Branding is the assurance you provide to the person you want to influence. It is the guarantee that you will continually deliver what you promise, and that your product and/or service will do what you say about it every single time. The goal of branding is to elicit a positive emotional response from the market. It is useful when the customer perceives your service or product to be the best in the market, and it allows you to convince the customer of your value without overtly asking them to buy your products and/or services.

What thoughts and feelings do you have when you think of Starbucks, Disney, or Kraft Macaroni and Cheese? Your opinions won't be based solely on what these companies say their brand is. Instead, your experience determines your feelings about them. The critical concept that your customers' experiences are often more important than what you deliver is the key to top influencer brands.

A brand is a personality. While the market ultimately determines a brand's persona, social enterprises and individuals develop their brand based on core values, intention for playing a part for the greater good as well as quality product and services. Positioning your brand to codify the value your brand offers and delivering your promise is imperative to your brand's success. Otherwise, your target market will determine how your brand is perceived. For example, you may want your market to recognize your brand as the upscale provider of experiential retreats or the quality and reasonably priced retreats for locals. Each of these brands requires a very different messaging to its market.

BRAND EXPERIENCE

Brand experience includes all the impressions your customers gain from interactions with your company. How does your receptionist answer the phone? How courteous are your delivery truck drivers? Do your customers' purchases arrive on time, or better yet, before you promised delivery? Are they delighted with every touch point with your company? Will they return to buy again? Are they recommending you to their friends? Experiences strongly influence your brand image, which is often closely tied to brand reputation.

BRAND POSITIONING

Brand Positioning combines both concepts of branding and positioning. Brand positioning is the target market's perception with regards to you as an individual or as a company or product or service. One of the key points to note is that if you do not define your brand and present this definition to your target market, the market may brand you either favorably or non-favorably.

To ensure optimal brand positioning, we need to understand the relationship between consumer and industry, relational experience between employees, as well as between employees and consumers. We also need to focus on the ability to deliver consistently quality customer experience throughout the entire process.

The introduction, purchase, and consumption of services occur at different times. For example, purchasing insurance for your home, car, or yourself can occur annually. Thus, a subscription necessitates periodic reinforcement and interaction of brand promise with customers to re-emphasize that your customers matter to you.

Constant monitoring, planning, and delivering brand promise services are required to meet the needs created by fluctuating consumer demands. It is best to project a realistic and authentic image with no pretense of being much more than you and your product or service are.

To clearly define and communicate to everyone with a stake in the company, marketers often create a brand positioning mantra. The mantra is inclusive of your target market description, how your brand is unique along with what you stand for, a declaration of your unique value proposition and promise to your target market, the emotional benefits of your products or services, as well as the rationale that makes your brand trustworthy.

The first step in creating a brand positioning mantra is to identify points of difference from the other market players, purpose, mission, and the top emotional benefits that resonate with your target market. After reviewing and finalizing your elements, generate a simple mantra that is purpose-driven and communicates the psychological benefits that customers receive. When your brand demonstrates its core values consistently through actions, you or your product or service will garner the coveted position of a trusted partner.

ACTIVITY – CREATE YOUR BRAND POSITIONING STATEMENT

For each section, supply a "brief" response. It's important for you to be succinct in your answers. Precise, targeted messaging will become a theme throughout the process. Also, remember, take your time with this exercise, as it is the foundation on which we will build everything else in the process.

- » Describe your Target Market
- » Describe your Competition
- » Describe the Emotional Benefits your products, services, or ideas deliver
- » Explain why you are believable
- » Describe your UVP or USP (Unique Value Proposition or Unique Selling Proposition), and what makes you different
- » Explain why your USP/UVP is believable

THE PROCESS – DESIGN IT, BUILD IT, LIVE IT

In my work with clients that want to become influencers, we always start with a focus on Positioning and Branding. I coach them through a process that helps move them from an expert, to an authority, to an influencer. The process has three phases.

The first phase is the Design Phase. It is the foundation of your brand. We do a deep dive to create clarity in your message – who are you, what you have to say, and what it means for you and your tribe.

The second phase is the Build Phase or the implementation of your branding platform. Here, you create your promise and then over-deliver on it, providing a full immersion experience to your market that makes everyone in it feel special and understood.

The third phase is Living your Brand in your everyday life. It's how you show up – how you think, how you act, and how everyone sees you. It becomes your lifestyle, allowing you to step into full authenticity.

Each phase builds on the previous one. Hence, it's essential to give a proper amount of time and attention to each step. We will take a deeper dive into each step in the process as you delve further into the book.

You already know the first step of the Design Phase, What is it? We've reviewed what an influencer is, and we've defined marketing and branding terms that we will use in the coming chapters. Now we'll begin our deep dive into Who it is For.

"To be in business today, our most important job is to be head marketer for the brand called You."

– Tom Peters in Fast Company

"If your market shares your values, they will stay loyal to your brand."

– Unknown

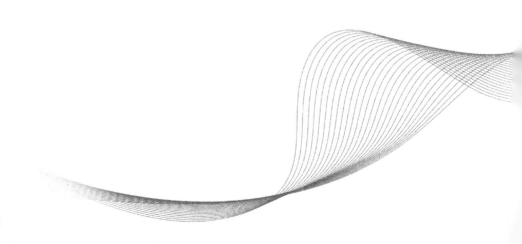

CHAPTER 2

WHO IS IT FOR?

Mia came into the newly christened "IT Success" and smiled at the activity going on in the offices. The last time she was here, the place had the quietness of a funeral parlor, and now it seemed more like a carnival. She jumped out of the way as someone with a laptop almost ran into her since the young man was walking and typing at the same time. Mia scurried down the hall before getting run over again and knocked lightly on the door. She heard a slightly frantic, "Come in!"

She entered and saw Amanda with her hair askew and half her shirt untucked from her slacks as she hung up her desk phone. Standing behind the desk, she glared at Mia and said, "This is your fault."

Mia stopped short and said, "Me? What did I do?"

"You turned me into a success."

"No, I guided you. You turned it into a success."

"Whatever!" Amanda sat down heavily. "You know I'm teasing. It has been a hectic day ... week ... the entire month."

"So, why did you call?" asked Mia.

"Two reasons," replied Amanda. "One, I want to be a little less hectic. Two, I've been asked to speak at the chamber of commerce next month. Forget that I am terrified of public speaking. I have no idea what to say to them. 'I help companies, and they like what we do' is not going to fill up twenty minutes."

Mia nodded and thought for a minute. Finally, she asked, "Do you remember when we first met, Amanda? You mentioned you wouldn't mind a couple of office locations throughout the state."

"I do. I was barely making ends meet here at the time."

"Yes, and then you revamped everything here. I don't mean the name which I love. I watched your people as I came in. They all move with a sense of purpose. They treat your clients like you did. You instilled in them your values and way of treating customers, and it shows. I think this opportunity to speak to the chamber of commerce is an ideal stepping-stone for you."

"Stepping-stone!" said Amanda in amazement. "It feels like a cinder block around my neck."

"No," said Mia, "it will help you to articulate how you became a success. Other businesspeople will hear how you did this. Bankers with money to lend successful businesses will hear how you became a success. In this day and age, if you are going to be a success, you cannot stay in the background."

Amanda asked, "Will you help me articulate all of that?"

Mia answered, "Of course."

Letting out a sigh, Amanda asked, "How about the craziness of running this place?"

"How's Steve doing with running the training you give your clients?" Mia asked.

"Fantastic. Steve hired an assistant," said Amanda.

"He's a sharp guy. Make him operations manager and take some of the day to day off you. You hired me to help. It's time to learn delegation and get ready to expand IT Success. Business leaders notice you in this town. Let's strike while the iron is getting hot!"

DESIGN PHASE

There is a ton of information out there about knowing your market, and there's a good reason many marketing experts write on this topic. Most companies, and moreover individuals, spend a lifetime trying to understand their market. The typical sequence new businesses use in defining their market is they create a product or service they know something about, and then they try to find people that want it. If they buy it, great! If they don't, it's back to the drawing board to create another something someone might want.

Create first and market later is the path most experts follow, someone who knows a lot about their craft, and not a lot about who might want it. People may or may not be interested in that expertise, and most aren't even aware there is specific expertise that exists. Occasionally, an expert becomes well-known for their knowledge of the something they offer. They become the authority in a particular area and become known for their in-depth knowledge of the product or services. Most people aren't necessarily excited by this deeper level of expertise, and those that are, are a focused market that continues to follow the brand because they want this exceptional expertise again and again.

For example, Whirlpool is one of the most reliable brands of household appliances. They are not only experts in making good washing machines, but they are also authorities in designing, delivering, and servicing a full range of appliances with excellent reviews and top placement in the market for many years.

If you flip this model and begin by finding a group of people that have something in common, which is something that you know about, then you are setting the foundation for influence marketing. Putting customers first takes on a whole new meaning in this context.

Let's take it one step further. If you segment this group of people into more precise sub-groups and obtain a deep understanding of the uniqueness of a particular sub-group, and offer expertise they want, now you are moving into a role of genius or thought leader, at least in the sub-group's eyes. If the sub-group, or tribe, fully identifies with you and sees you as a top authority, they will come back for more. If you consistently provide what they expect from you, they will be long-term customers, and you move into that elusive role of influencer. Now, you can use your expertise, your authority, and your brand experience to present new ideas and offer them new products and services that they willingly want to buy.

No one knew this level of influencer marketing better than Steve Jobs. He knew Apple's early adopter market better than anyone. Jobs said, "It's not our job to give customers what they want; it's to figure out what they are going to want before they do." Jobs liked to quote Henry Ford, "If I asked what they wanted they would have told me 'a faster horse!'" He said people don't know what they want until you show it to them.

Researching how focused market segmentation and continual performance branding works will help get you started on your path to becoming an authentic influencer. The ones that have figured it out are the ones that have a dominant market share, where both the provider and the customer are blissful in their partnership.

THE DESIGN PHASE – CREATING CLARITY IN YOUR MESSAGE

The Design Phase is the foundation to create your entire brand. Understanding fully who you are, who your marketing is, and where your market goes to get what you have to offer are the building blocks of your foundation. It is the upfront research needed to create real clarity in your message.

WHO ARE YOU?

The Design Phase starts with who you are. Defining yourself with clarity and creating your attractive brand persona is essential to establishing your brand. How others perceive you is vital because people's perception determines your reputation. Having clarity about who you are makes sharing your persona much easier. Keep in mind that communicating dry facts will most likely lose people's attention. When you share your authentic self with your audience, you will connect with your audience at a deeper level because people like those who are genuine. You oversee your brand persona, as long as you take the wheel.

There are no rules that say you have to share all the personal details about yourself. It is vital to share your values and facts related to your products and services. For example, you can share your struggles and messes in your journey to success. The key is to share facts because lies get revealed, especially in today's technology world. You want your own integrity and values.

ESTABLISH YOUR VALUES

Your values are who you are if you look at yourself realistically and without judgment. Most of us have a few top values that were first taking form when we were young children and then modified or solidified as we test the waters in our growth to maturity. Understanding what your top values are is the key to crafting your "Message." They are the basis for how you will communicate with your market, and more importantly, how they will identify with what you have to say.

ACTIVITY – VALUES ASSESSMENT
[https://success.divyaparekh.com/values-assessment/][1]

If you believe you already know what your values are, you might want to validate them by taking this assessment. You never know; it's possible one might pop up you didn't realize was a critical one. If you aren't clear on what they are, then you surely will want to take the assessment.

This step might be the most important one in designing your brand. It is the foundation for it, so I recommend that you don't skip it or go through the assessment too quickly. Give it time to marinate, and make sure you are genuinely committed to your top three values, ensuring they are the ones that have been key for most of your life.

---

1   If you desire to know what kind of an influencer you are, take the quiz at https://success.divyaparekh.com/values-assessment/.

They are the ones you stand firm for and nothing will dissuade you to cross a line.

Check in with someone that knows you deeply, to see if your values resonate with them in who you are. I have a close friend that I call my "mirror" friend. We agree that we are going to be deeply honest with each other so we can always understand how others perceive us. If you have a close friend, colleague, or family member, ask if they would mind if you bounced a few things off of them. I want to warn you that this cannot be someone critical of you; they must be a trusted person that would go to the end of the earth with you. If you have such a person in your circles, treasure them. If not, hire a coach. They are trained to tell the truth in a supportive and caring way.

Challenge yourself, because you will interweave these values into everything you do. They will be how you design, deliver, and live your brand as a top influencer.

My top three values are mindfulness, nurturing relationships, and wisdom. I can trace the beginnings of these values back to my early childhood. I've always loved meditating, which leads me to mindfulness. I learned how to cultivate and nurture relationships from my dad. As for wisdom, I've always had a voracious curiosity to learn, and there are no boundaries in my passion for knowledge. As I grew up and experienced the world, I solidified these values by practicing and experiencing how they brought me joy.

When I worked in the corporate world, I had many challenging opportunities. It would have been easy to become bitter and defensive, like many of my colleagues. However, my values allowed me to prosper and even thrive in my work. I developed deep relationships with my colleagues. My most profound relationships I developed with our clients. I always gave with expectations for us all to succeed. I saw that we were connected, rather than competitive, and that we were all working for the good of the whole, which at that time in my life was to bring lifesaving drugs to people with unmet needs. I was able to get things done that others couldn't because the people I had developed excellent relationships with trusted me and wanted to work with me. I was always willing to go to bat for them, and they helped me in return.

ACTIVITY – VALUE JOURNEY

> » After you take the assessment, answer the following questions in your journal.
> » What are your top three values? When did you first start identifying with them?
> » Write down a few brief situations you remember from your childhood that show how each of your top three values were established in your thoughts or actions. How have these values changed or solidified as you as you experienced life, and why? Jot down a few ideas on how they've changed over time and what caused the changes.
> » Finally, how are they showing up in your daily life today? Jot down a few examples of how you continue to see these values in how you interact with others, or how you react to something that challenges your beliefs.

Now you have your top three values and a good understanding of how you assimilated them. These are the basis for who you are, what your brand will communicate, and how your tribe will connect with you.

SWOT ANALYSIS

The next step is to implement a SWOT analysis. The analysis helps you cut through loads of information and discern relevant strengths, weaknesses, opportunities, and threats. The resulting self-knowledge will help you understand what you represent, the offers that are unique to you, and areas that you could work on.

ACTIVITY – SWOT ANALYSIS

SWOT analysis is exclusive to each person or business. An honest evaluation of you and your business allows you to build a comprehensive personal and business success framework.

1. SWOT analysis will be unique to each brand, whether it be an individual, company, or small business. Usually, it is helpful to review Strengths, Weaknesses, Opportunities, Threats from an individual or organizational perspective as well as from the target market's perspective.
2. Create a table of two columns and two rows.
3. Label each square: Strengths, Weaknesses, Opportunities, Threats

» Strengths: Strengths includes knowledge, skills, experiences, resources, as well as the support you have concerning other players in the same niche. For instance, storytelling is a strength for a speaker.

» Weaknesses: Weaknesses include tasks that you can improve upon and skills and knowledge that you can build upon. For example, procrastination would fall under the category of weaknesses.

» Opportunities: Opportunities are external because they are related to the environment and people around you. The examination of the external factor helps you discover how they affect you or business and play a role in the generation of growth and profit opportunities. For example, when someone goes on a sabbatical, it creates a possibility for you to take the initiative and do something new.

» Threats: Like opportunities, threats are external too because they are related to the environment and people around you. For example, changing consumer trends can affect you or your business drastically. We see the popularity of online shopping severely impacting retail stores.

4. Under each label, make a list of at least five things that apply to each label, relevant to you and your business or brand.

5. Draw conclusions. These are not solutions, but rather a general theme in the form of a succinct statement that

umbrellas all of the things you listed. You will have four statements.

6. Now create a list of actionable strategies using your strengths and weaknesses to take advantage of opportunities and minimize threats.

PASSIONS

Your brand should be representative of your purpose and passions.

ACTIVITY – WHAT ARE YOU PASSIONATE ABOUT?

Answer the following question to determine your purpose and your passions. Consider why each passion is so relatable, and how does it make your life memorable. If you focus only on your work passions, like wanting to increase company profits by 10%, your market will perceive you as dry and dull. When you personalize the work passion with an inspiring intention, then you connect deeply with your present audience and attract a new audience. One good example would be to increase profits by 30% so that you could create more jobs for the local market. Additionally, you can personalize your brand with the causes you support. For example, if you are good at soccer, you could donate your time as well as sponsor a local soccer team. Another example will be to support young teenage girls if you believe in women empowerment.

1. What do you care about and why?
2. What drives you and why?
3. What are you wildly passionate about and why?
4. What do you love and why?
5. What do you hate (or if that word is a bit strong, what do you most dislike) and why?
6. What gives you a sense of fulfillment?

It's vital to know what you dislike as much as what you like, so you know when you are out of sync with your values. This understanding will help you to turn away potential tribe members that are not in alignment with you. Trust me; it's better to leave them behind now than wasting your energy on them later.

WHO'S YOUR MARKET?

Most of you already have a market unless you are starting a new business or have started a new career or job. If you already have a market, what do you know about it? Let's look at some parameters you should use in your criteria.

SEGMENT YOUR MARKET

Market segmentation is how you divide up your market to have a clearer picture of your customers. You have to ask questions to understand and know your prospective customer. These questions address the demographics, desires, problems, psychographics, and behavioral attributes of the prospect. This information gives you the flexibility to target your advertising, message, and services to specific sub-markets. It can also power your product and service development by learning what the different segments need, like men vs. women, or millennials vs. baby boomers.

Geographic Segmentation – business is determined by geographical areas whether they are cities, counties, states, regions, or countries. People's needs vary depending on where they live. Advertising and marketing are also going to be different depending on the location.

Demographic Segmentation – utilizes categories like age, race, religion, gender, family size, ethnicity, occupation, income, and education. Most products and services are designed to target specific demographic sections of society. The interests of an employed 50-year-old divorced mom would be different from that of a married mom in her 20's.

Firmographic Segmentation – occurs if you are a business-to-business company. It applies to organizations instead of individual consumers. Businesses selling to other companies want to know things like company size and the number of employees because selling to small businesses would require an entirely different marketing strategy and communication than selling to enterprise organizations.

Behavioral Segmentation – divides markets based on the buying patterns of customers like usage frequency, lifestyle, and brand loyalty. For example, millennials are more apt to rent an apartment in a hip multi-use community than buy a house 30 minutes from downtown.

Behavioral Segmentation requires a very sharp insight on consumer behavior and is key to influencer marketing.

Psychographic Segmentation – involves understanding the problems, interests, personality characteristics, values, perspectives, and routines of your target market. The information equips marketers to provide customer-centric products and services with an emphasis on experience.

ACTIVITY – MARKET SEGMENTATION

Take some time now to list each type of market segmentation and define your market according to the specific items in each category. Start with Geographic and work your way through each segmentation section. You will be creating a "personality" for your market that will be more and more unique as you further identify how they are segmented.

ACTIVITY – PERSONAL SEGMENTATION

Now create the same list for you personally or for your business. What do you have in common with your market? Circle the items that overlap. How many overlaps are there? Many? Hopefully! A few? Time to explore why.

If you are a mismatch with your market, you'll likely not understand them well enough to engage them unless you are a world class marketer who knows how to market any product or service to any market segment. You know, the person who can sell ice to an Eskimo.

If you overlap a lot, it's much easier to figure out what they need, because you probably need it too. Consider the creators of ENO hammocks. An ENO hammock is a lightweight, high-strength hammock that holds up to use and abuse. It is easy to clip its aluminum carabiners to any solid anchor point, and it is compatible with most hammock suspension systems. It packs down to the size of a grapefruit and has become the most popular hammock sold to outdoor enthusiasts in the past ten years.

Eagle Nest Outfitters was founded in 1999 by a group of guys from Florida who traveled the music festival and community gatherings circuit up and down the East Coast, selling hammocks out of their ramshackle minivan. They shared the life their market lived, and by grassroots interaction, they learned not only what their market wanted, but also, how they experienced the hammocks, and what was important to their lifestyle. That started their business and now ENO products has 2,000 locations in 13 countries.

ACTIVITY – BRAND LONGEVITY

What other companies can you identify that have brand longevity from early on and then went into owning a major market share? Research these companies and jot the steps they took in your branding journal. How did they start and what was their product or service? Were they part of their market? How did they determine the gap in the market and create the product or service? How were their demographics similar to their market's? How did they grow? What changed? What remained the same? Did they become performance branders? Influencers? If you were them, what would you do next?

BRAND CONNECTION

» People choose certain brands because of their feeling of connectivity with the brand. A highly relatable brand makes your audience have:

» A sense of personal worth. (They deserve a Mercedes Benz because they only buy a car with quality engineering and want others to know that about them.)

» Validation of their beliefs and values and thereby, psychic satisfaction. (They believe in what you believe. For example, Starbucks funnels profits to its foundation. The Starbucks foundation supported non-profit organizations by giving millions of dollars to them. Additionally, they invest in the communities that are suppliers of its coffee, tea, and cocoa.)

» A product or service that serves them the best. (American Express's emphasis on being a brand with exceptional customer service is matched with the delivery of actual customer service. Recently, I received a text alert, an alert call as well as an email alert with regards to fraudulent charges. After I talked with the customer representatives, they assured me that not only would I not pay for any of the fraudulent charges made on my behalf, but that they also would pursue the matter. The next day after I receive the alerts, a few vendors started calling me with regards to the charges. I jotted down the phone numbers and called American Express customer service. They asked me to stay on the line and called the vendors, letting them know that American Express was looking into the matter. Moreover, after that, the vendors stopped calling me. With their great customer service, not only do they have me for life as a customer but also as a fan who is sharing about them through my book.)

» A sharp image of themselves being a successful person because successful people are using it. (Your VP reads The Wall Street Journal, and so do you.)

» Help for day-to-day problems. (Google provides the largest search engine.)

» Fulfillment of their needs. (Air France Airline is known for high comfort during transatlantic air travel.)

» A sense of belonging because you are a part of a community comprised of like-minded people. (Star Trek fans mirror the actions of other fans and follow the crowd with the utmost enthusiasm.)

» A reflection of how other people perceive them. (Cool people purchase iPhones.)

ACTIVITY – BRANDING CONNECTION

Make a list of the ways your audience will connect with you. What is unique about your relationship in their eyes that will make them want to come back for more? Please include in your list numerous ways you can reach out to them, providing more than your primary offering. What else do they want in the form

of connection? How do they want to experience what you are selling, or saying?

The connection is key to providing an unforgettable experience, and memorable experiences keep your audience engaged. Thus, the deeper you understand how to connect, over and over again, the more loyal your tribe will be.

BRANDING MISCONCEPTIONS

Before we move on, I want to share a few branding myths or misconceptions I've discovered in my years of working with influencers. I share them because they are easy hooks that can trigger you into moving in the wrong direction. It is critical to be aware of the possible pitfalls. Awareness drives success!

The Product Misconception – *The first misconception is that the right product is ultimately going to create a good brand, that products and brands are the same, and if you focus on developing the best products, you will eventually have the brand that you need for your business to grow.*

While the right products can be very successful, the combination of excellent products with great Branding is vital for influencers.

The Lottery Misconception – *Another misconception is that many people think they need to have a fantastic brand right at the start if they are going to have one at all and that some companies are lucky and hit the mark with a trendy message.* As you grow and learn, similarly will your brand. Be flexible, resilient, open to change, and keep your ear to the ground.

The Identity System Misconception – *According to the identity system misconception, a company will have its brand when it has its logo, packaging, business cards, website, and letterheads in place.* As you well know by now, considerable upfront research is required before you pick your color scheme or tag line.

The Right of Passage Misconception – *The Right of Passage misconception is that many people believe that their business is too small to start with branding.* I would venture to say that as soon as you know what you want to offer, it's time to begin the Design Phase activities before you even test your product or service.

The Induction in the Industry Misconception – *And finally, many people believe that the work that goes into branding is only required when they are first starting.* The truth is that even after a company builds a strong following, continuing to research and tweak your brand image is necessary to keep it on track.

All of these are misunderstandings of what Branding is, why it's needed, and how to build a brand, and together we are going to demystify all of this.

To illustrate, I'll share a story about my early days of establishing my business. At the time, I had a business partner that was seeking similar goals. We both left the corporate world after obtaining a coaching certification and incorporating our businesses. We designed what we thought was a great two-day leadership workshop for professional women. We created the outline and wrote our scripts. We made slides and workbooks and put together activity kits for all the participants. We booked a meeting room that held up to 100 people at a local hotel and arranged for coffee and drinks throughout the day, and lunch delivered from a local sandwich restaurant. We created "branding" (i.e., a logo and color scheme) and used it on the slides, on the workbooks, and for the marketing. Then we "marketed" our program to women in the corporate world we knew. We waited anxiously for our "friends in need" to sign up. After all, who wouldn't want to attend such a great program!

We waited and waited, and then we started to panic. Only four women signed up, and one dropped out before the first day of the workshop. Should we cancel? Should we delay and market more? How could this be happening after all the work we put into creating this incredible workshop?

We couldn't hide from reality; we did something vastly wrong, but we didn't know what it was. Fast forward to today, five years later, and after studying and learning from the best marketers in the business, we finally can look back at what we did wrong.

ACTIVITY – WHAT WE DID WRONG

In your journal, jot down at least three things you can identify that we did wrong. Look back on the activities we've already completed and see if there's anything we skipped. Look at the Branding Misconceptions and include any of those you see from my experience.

As I look at it now with Monday morning quarterbacking, the most glaring thing we did wrong was that we led with the product first. We also spent too much time on logos and content before we understood our market and our brand. We did not do any Design Phase work. We knew we shared many values with our market, but we didn't carve them out about ourselves, and we certainly didn't do any market research to see if they were in alignment with our target audience. We assumed that since we were in their shoes when we worked in the corporate world, we had a clear picture of who they were and what they wanted or needed. We also didn't think about how they would feel sitting in a room learning from two women who used to be their peers and their bosses.

We lumped them all into one bucket and didn't do any market segmentation. Since we didn't know the critical values and market segmentation, we didn't use any of this in our marketing content. We didn't nurture them at all before we hit them with the hard sell – come to our workshop. In retrospect, it's pretty amazing we had the three people that showed up!

I think the key to me understanding all of this, and then knowing it well enough to now write about it and coach people to become great influencers, is that at some point I realized I didn't know enough to be successful. I did what I have always done – I sought out people who were authorities on the subject. I hired marketing coaches and bought their online programs. I read their books and attended conferences, workshops, and retreats, where we studied and practiced together. Some of the best influencers out there – top online marketers, prominent keynote speakers, well-known authors, and famous podcasters – mentored me. I studied everything they had to share. I "practiced" and failed, and I "practiced" and had some success, and then I failed again, and had a few more victories, until here I am today, with an in-depth knowledge of how the best get it done.

I'm sharing all of this now because I don't want you to have to spend the time, money, or energy I did on a hit or miss journey of what it takes to be a top influencer. I've compiled it all into this book, and I want it to be easier for you to get there than it was for me. I'm sharing what I know to support you to become a top influencer, in whatever "market" you choose. Know that it makes my heart full to see my clients find success.

Now on to the next part of our journey – Why is it important?

"Every great dream begins with a dreamer. Always remember, you have within you the strength, the patience, and the passion to reach for the stars to change the world."

– Harriet Tubman

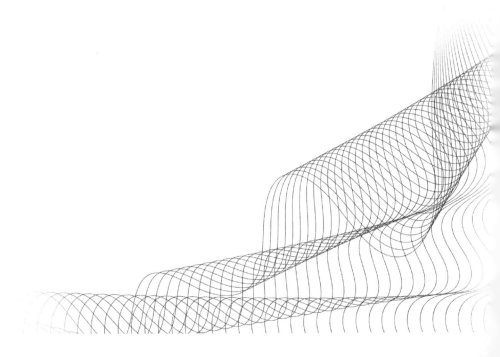

CHAPTER 3

WHY IS IT IMPORTANT?

Standing at the back of the room, Mia listened as Amanda concluded her speech to the chamber of commerce. They had gone through a great deal of work in the past month articulating what Amanda believed about herself and her business. She gave practice speeches to her small group of employees that helped Amanda get used to public speaking and to hone her content so she was saying exactly what she wanted to say. Mia could see that what Amanda spoke about resonated with her employees. It helped Amanda realize that she guided her business and vision with her values. As she continued to practice, the passion of her speech became more natural and not as forced as it was when they started practicing. Mia listened to that passion now as Amanda got to the end of her speech.

"Nobody is more surprised than me to be up here talking to you all tonight. I started out wanting to help companies who had major issues with the information technology they utilized. As I put together the words you heard tonight about how I got the idea and then plunged into owning my own business, I realized that offering companies a service – an exceptional service at that," she said with a grin and an appreciative chuckle from the audience, "was the vehicle to do what I really wanted. I wanted to give people a break from the craziness we all encounter every day, whether it be with work, family, or other things we are involved in."

Amanda glanced at her notes. "I wanted to create an environment where a company could explain their needs to someone who would listen – I mean actively listen to their issues – and then come up with a solution to meet their problems. There would be no bait and switch or needless upselling. My company would carry about our obligations with a sense of honor and go back to old-fashioned values like the customer is first.

"The one thing I have learned in business is that sometimes it is a chicken and egg approach we have to do. I knew my IT plan was good, but I needed to have more people use it. I learned to do some marketing that reached out to businesses of all sizes. Several local businesses tried us and enjoyed the experience and became the best advocates I could have for my business. I learned to communicate with them through Facebook and other media. It didn't take long to go from coming up with innovative concepts nobody else was using to having someone manage the day-to-day operations so I could strategically continue growing the business."

Firmly picking up her notes and stuffing them in her pocket, Amanda said, "Thank you for letting me talk to you this evening. You have no idea how this scared me. The president of the chamber of commerce asked me to speak on why IT Success lived up to its name and became so successful. Know what your customers want, tell them they will get it from you, and back it up each time!

"Thank you for your attention, and for giving me the chance to talk to all of you. Speaking to you wasn't as scary as I thought. Have a great evening!"

Mia felt a bit of pride as Amanda got a rousing ovation from the crowd. The young woman had a knack for engaging people. Mia began to think what the next step should be for Amanda and IT Success.

WHY IT'S IMPORTANT TO YOUR AUDIENCE

We've done a great deal of work on who your message is for, but we haven't touched on why it's important to them. The question I always ask people is, "Does your product, service or message solve an important problem for your audience?"

I have a tool I use when I'm trying to understand the root of a problem. I ask myself six questions about the problem I am solving for them. Let's use it with the problem you are solving for your audience.

ACTIVITY – AM I SOLVING A PROBLEM THEY REALLY CARE ABOUT?

For each question, write it down, and then briefly and succinctly detail how each question relates to your audience's problem and why. Add what their primary emotions are around that particular answer.

For example, let's use a common problem my clients have: They are an expert in their craft, but not well-known enough that people perceive them as an influencer.

1. Is it Clear-Cut? Yes, because the problem is well-known and unambiguous. They feel intense and stressed because they know for sure they have the problem.
2. Is it Urgent? Yes, it is urgent because they are not happy with the way things are. They want to make a massive impact as well as build a lifestyle that gives them freedom. Since that is not the case, they feel desperate, overwhelmed, and stuck.
3. Is it Significant? Yes, it is significant because it costs them joy and freedom. They are losing precious time and the richness of the relationships that they could have.
4. Is it Relentless? Yes, the problem is persistent and pervasive. If your business is not growing and if you are not making the impact you want to, the passion starts drying up. What was once a pleasure becomes a burden to carry.
5. Is it Costly? Yes, because it costs lost time, energy, and money. Bear in mind that you will have to replenish finite resources.
6. Is it Obvious? Yes, it is glaringly obvious because you can shout at the top of your voice and if nobody hears you, you are not making an impact.

If you are struggling to answer any of these questions, it's possible you aren't solving a big problem. Many successful businesses solve problems with solutions that aren't life-changing (think Coca-Cola), and if you are super innovative and ahead of your time, your market may not even know they have this problem to solve. Remember, Henry

Ford, inventing the automobile for a market that was asking for a faster horse?

Most influencers are breaking barriers in areas that are big problems for people. If you are still struggling with the answers, try the problem solving exercise with an influential product, service, or message you know well. This additional exercise might help you find ways to understand your answers easier. In my experience, it is helpful to go back and pull out each emotion you wrote down. These emotions are great words to use in describing your audience's pain point. Most people "buy" on emotion. This point is the crux of why your offering is essential to your audience. Understanding your audience's problem on a profound emotional basis will magnetize your message, drawing people to you, your branding, and your solution.

WHY IS BRANDING IMPORTANT?

Branding is what makes a lasting impression on your audience, allowing them to know what to expect from you. It outlines "why" you exist and is an idealistic view of what you want to become to your audience, exhibiting the values and behaviors you'll use to get them what they want.

Strong brand identity will help acquire followers, and it builds credibility and trust. A strong brand message will influence your current and prospective clients' response to your products, services, and ideas. Customers like brands that they share values with, and those that garner an emotional response build customer loyalty.

When they recognize and remember you, they will come back for more, and if you've hit the mark, they will influence others to follow you as well. Therefore, market research is a critical first step in brand development!

As an added benefit, responsive and robust branding makes advertising easier. You keep everything within the design criteria, that is your factual foundation, and each new campaign creates continued growth in your audience.

We study to create positioning, authority, and influence. Within that umbrella, we scrutinize prospects, colleagues, upper management, bosses, teammates, people that we know, people that we understand, and people that we meet. Ultimately, the common thread in all of this is people. It's about people wanting more joy in their lives and about experiencing life at a heightened level in terms of learning, understanding, growth, achieving success, mastering their craft, relaxing, enjoying life, and finding peace of mind. Our role as an influencer is to bring it to them with ease and excitement for more.

What do we draw upon to keep our excitement going? What keeps us between the lines of authenticity? Where does our "Why" come from?

It comes from the people who have influenced us, and our own experiences practicing the lessons learned from our past. My friend and fellow coach likes to say, "It is who we become as a result of the experience, not the experience itself, which is most valuable." While we want to provide an excellent experience for our tribe, what we are really reaching for is the joy and happiness that results from the experience.

I recall many people who influenced me, whether it was a five-minute interaction or a long- term relationship – some positively and some negatively. The experiences taught me whose footsteps I wanted to follow and whose I didn't. As I think about all these influencers, many come to mind. Here are a couple of my influencers, with a few insights on how they still influence me today in my life and my brand.

Sister Olivia only had to smile and ask me gently to do something for her, and I would do it. There were a few bullies that would try to push me to do something mean to some of the other less fortunate girls, but I would stand my ground and not succumb to their taunts. I learned early on that kindness ruled.

Nans, my long-time California friend, with her open heart and unending confidence in me, effortlessly persuaded me to walk in the arena of multilevel marketing in my early 20's, despite my fear and skepticism of this new entrepreneurial world.

I learned that honest, caring human beings who live their lives by their values might not grow your circle by hundreds or thousands, but they will give you the followers who will walk the end of the earth for you. Loving and caring for others cuts through the noise and provides a consistent message across the board. When you speak your truth and are transparent, it is much easier than developing a persona that is not the original you. People see you as genuine. Hence, they are attracted to that, but they are also a bit in awe of how transparent you are. Do that in today's world, and I promise that you will stand out in a crowd of manipulative marketing.

What makes a brand iconic defies our understanding because people's hearts control the response. I realized in my childhood that when someone genuinely cares for people, they are often automatically influential. The concept was reinforced and validated throughout life as I experienced it both internally and with others. When I accept myself with love and release expectations, I experience the freedom that fuels my drive to continue my journey. Similarly, when I know people genuinely care, their flaws and honesty that sometimes hurts do not invoke resentment because I know exactly where they are coming from. The common thread is to have congruence in our values and messages. This consistency allows me to weed out the people, actions, thoughts, and beliefs that slow me down and stop me from moving forward. My message is true to who I am, so it comes out with ease in all that I do.

WHY IS INFLUENCING IMPORTANT?

Remember that influence is the power you have to compel others to act or behave a certain way. The goal is to persuade them to see things your way. It is not to manipulate them, which is why defining values and declaring integrity are two of the most important parts of designing your brand.

The ability to motivate others to achieve an important objective or to buy a certain product is good but influencing such that everyone feels like they "won" in the end is a honed practice. Developing reciprocity, where your customers feel they received an equal or better return on what they invested, is key to building your influence.

"You" as an influencer, is part of your brand. In fact, it is a significant part of your brand. How you are perceived is as vital as how well your product performs or how well your ideas pan out. Have you ever asked anyone how you are perceived?

One of the most reliable ways to find out if you are perceived differently than how you see yourself is to engage in a 360-degree assessment. Corporations usually use a 360-degree assessment to obtain feedback from an employee's colleagues, team members, and supervisors and then compare those answers to the employee's self-evaluation. The primary goal is to identify any gaps between the scores from self-evaluation and the scores from the others. Self-awareness is often the biggest problem with leaders, so it's the perfect place to start when embarking on leadership development. The same holds for branding and positioning. It is super important to understand how your audience perceives you, your brand, and your message.

ACTIVITY – HOW ARE YOU PERCEIVED VS. HOW YOU SEE YOURSELF

Short of purchasing a formal 360-degree assessment, you can easily create one on your own. Design a small "focus group" comprised of people in your target market and ask for feedback from them.

I've made a mistake more times than I can remember of asking the "wrong" group or person advice on something I'm creating. If they are not really in my target market, they will not respond accordingly, and now you are going down a rabbit hole of misinformation and mismatched messaging.

For this focus group, create a set of 5-10 questions about your message that you want to test. Here are a few examples that I've used in testing how my market perceives my business, but I encourage you to create several that are unique to you and your brand.

1. Which of these messages do you most connect within your desire to be an influencer?
   » Make your message a movement.
   » Receiving begins with giving.

> » Mobilize your message.
> » Mindfulness works everywhere.
>
> 2. What are other people saying about you?
>   » You deliver what you promise.
>   » You genuinely care about others.
>   » Your expertise is unique.
>   » Your process works.

Recently I shared a post on Facebook about this guy who used his Ph.D. degree to clean up his childhood lake. A lady named, Nicole, commented rather snippily that our lakes are clean enough, and that we should spend our money on other problems. My first reaction was to defend the post and argue Nicole's point because runoff from farming was leading to massive kills in the Gulf of Mexico. Moreover, what about Flint, Michigan's water supply?

Instead, I messaged her privately and asked why she thought this was a bad idea. We got to talking and, amazingly, she began to soften some. At first, she hadn't realized the guy was talking about lakes in Peru and Bolivia, not the U.S., and she agreed there is a severe problem in other parts of the world. Then after further talking, she decided that if we don't have clean water, the repercussions in creating other issues are massive. We talked about Flint not having clean drinking water and how families are affected. We discussed how the people along the Gulf that rely on tourism for their livelihood are struggling with the red tide that has kept people from going on vacation there. We ended up having a lovely chat and quite possibly created a budding friendship.

While this situation did not bring me any business, it pinpoints how "living" your brand should be natural if you create a brand that is true to who you are. If you pretend or put on a persona that does not represent "you," it will not work. Acting within the design criteria of your values should be easy. People need to know that you are going to be who you purport to be, and not some fake persona you created to get them to buy in.

DEFINING HOW YOU WANT TO BE SEEN

Rather than leave it to chance, it will boost your brand if you know how you want to be seen and then show up that way. I like to pause before I enter a conversation or a meeting to remind myself that I am showing up with integrity, and that I will defend my values if they get challenged. It settles me and gives me a calm mindset. I mainly make sure I do this if I know I'm entering a challenging situation. Defining how you want others to see you, and then reiterating that idea as you walk throughout your daily life will solidify your brand and gives you the power to be who you want to be.

ACTIVITY – HOW I WANT TO BE SEEN

Reflect on the activities we've completed so far, especially the Values, Passion, and 360 Review. In three brief bullet points, write how you want to be seen. Feel free to see this as an ongoing exercise since it may change as you dive deeper into understanding who you are as an influencer.

WHY IT'S IMPORTANT TO INVEST IN YOUR BRAND

If you've made it this far, you have invested in creating your brand. When I think of investing, I include how much time, money, and especially energy I give to create the desired outcome. I can recall several times when I spent considerable time, money, and energy that didn't get my desired outcome. Looking back, I can see the reason it didn't work. I distributed my attention to the various messages, and I ended up not doing the design work to create that focus.

I am often amazed at how many people are unsatisfied in their work, and yet they aren't doing anything concrete to shift their situation. They keep doing the same thing and getting the same results, and their frustrations and the complaining continues to elevate. What's more, they have every opportunity to change, but they still don't take the initiative to transform for the better. They can easily choose to follow others ahead of them, such as great leaders, authors, business owners, influencers, but they decide not to invest in their future success.

Initially, I branded my business in several areas, and if I were to mention all of them here, it would be a book on its own. I was pretty much all over the map, offering anyone whatever it was they needed if it was in my undefined wheelhouse. My business coach got more and more frustrated with me because I was spending my energy, effort, time, and money on different ventures and not getting any results. I was saying "yes" to everything and always running after the next shiny thing. She advised me to narrow my focus and do those things well. As I changed my scattered attention to laser focus on my target audience, the focus moved the needle. I began consistently sharing the same message across a few deliberate platforms, targeted to my audience.

Soon people started identifying with my brand and me. They were engaging and connecting and seeking me out rather than the other way around! I remind myself of this all the time, that with structure comes freedom.

From this day forward, shift your thinking and join me in our constant up-leveling of ourselves. I think of it as relentless, continuous improvement with unprecedented rewards. Kudos to you if you've been completing all the activities in this book. By doing the upfront work, you will have a clear focus of how you want to show up, and you will have reams of information and data to rely upon as you continue to hone your brand.

IF YOU DON'T, THEY WILL

Market share is used to determine the size of a company concerning other players in the same industry. You can evaluate the market share by dividing the company's sales over a definitive time period by the total sales of the industry over the same period.

The point is that there is a relatively finite number of sales possible, and if you don't capture them, someone else will. There are a limited number of people you can influence. If someone else has a stronger brand and is better at persuasion than you, they will draw people instead of you.

I've seen this play out in the corporate world. Over the years, I've had good bosses, OK bosses, and a few horrible bosses. The work we did was fast paced, intellectually challenging, and because it was development work, problems peppered the work. My team was motivated to go the extra mile when we had a good boss. We wanted to deliver because we saw how it affected our boss, and she shared with us positive public rewards. She used to tell us her father taught her to praise publicly and correct privately, and that was new to us. She also challenged us with leadership tasks. While our plates were already overflowing, we were motivated to take on this extra work because she saw future leaders in all of us. She was very persuasive with her positive attitude even though we knew she also faced difficult challenges at her level.

Of course, we got the work done for the OK bosses, but I had to find validation elsewhere – from our clients, other team members, or the people we delivered to internally. Work was still challenging, but there was a low sort of feeling in the group. We didn't have as much fun solving problems and we grew to expect nothing much from our blasé boss.

When we had a horrible boss, the entire team was snarky. We struggled to be a cohesive group. People teamed up and complained a lot, and the most miserable, least resilient people left the company. That may have been a good thing if we were able to fill their positions, but we were on a hiring freeze. Even though these people were toxic culturally, we desperately needed their technical expertise and hours on the job.

Like most things in corporate, soon enough we had yet another boss, and things changed for the better again. As I look back, and since I've studied persuasion, influence, and branding, I can see the telltale signs of the excellent boss' brand. She operated naturally out of integrity, and she indeed saw the potential in all of us. She genuinely cared about how we developed our careers, and she was quite influential as she moved up further in the company. She didn't let her peers sway how she showed up for us by often sticking her neck out to shield us or make our lives easier.

The horrible boss was operating with a sense of scarcity. He was very competitive and was always looking out for his career, and never seemed to care much about the rest of us, except of course, his one or two favorites that fed his ego. He also had a brand, and he was quite influential, but it wasn't a brand most people would choose to follow, and the influence was full of fear-mongering and shame.

ACTIVITY – POSITIVE AND NEGATIVE INFLUENCERS

Choose one person who is or was a positive influencer in your life. They can be someone you know now, knew in your past, or is someone well-known.

Jot down three values you think they operate from.

What are their strengths?

What are their weaknesses?

How do they overcome threats?

How do they take advantage of opportunities by leveraging their strengths?

How do they take advantage of opportunities by improving their weaknesses?

What are they passionate about?

What do they love?

What do they hate (or dislike immensely)?

Now choose a person that is a negative influencer.

What three values do they operate from?

What are their strengths?

What are their weaknesses?

How do they overcome threats?

How do they take advantage of opportunities by leveraging their strengths?

How do they take advantage of opportunities by improving their weaknesses?

What are they passionate about?

What do they love?

What do they hate (or dislike immensely)?

The more you practice seeing these traits in others, the clearer yours will become, and the more adept you will be at quickly pegging someone you meet at who they are.

As we continue to hone the Design of our Brand, it's also vital to know where your people go to get what you are dishing out. In the next chapter, we'll explore where they are hanging out and how you can get access to them.

"Start finding future clients before you have anything to sell them. Get to know these people as friends, not potential customers."

– Keith Ferrazzi

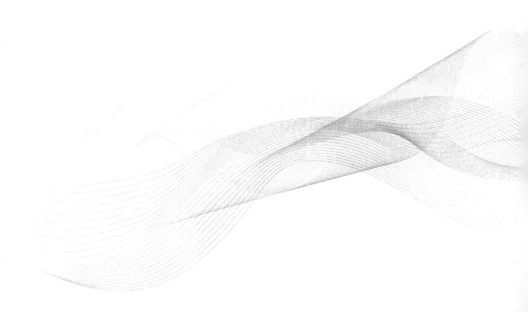

CHAPTER 4

WHERE DO THEY GET IT?

Walking into the auditorium at the Franchise Conference, Amanda was amazed at how many people were there. She decided to attend after researching the best ways to establish more locations for IT Success in the tri-state area, realizing that franchising was a great way to expand without having to invest all the money up front, and she didn't have to hire managers for each location.

For a conference with 450 attendees, she thought this was a great way to share her story and to pitch to a group of people looking to buy into a successful brand by owning a franchise. She realized she hadn't wasted her time on promoting her appearance here for the past three weeks when the conference committee offered her a spot after the scheduled speaker backed out. It usually took a year to get on the agenda, and Amanda only decided on trying the franchise route three months earlier. Now, here she was competing with the likes of McDonald's, Wendy's, Advanced Auto Parts, Dell, and other large companies.

As her business began to grow, Amanda recently launched three more offices in neighboring towns, and they all had signs of being a success. Once again, Amanda promoted Steve to what they decided to call a regional manager. That meant he made sure all four existing offices ran well and were consistent in how they treated customers and solved their IT problems. Now on to the next phase of expansion!

Amanda had spent a great deal of the past years networking with other business owners who were expanding their businesses. This exploration led her to groups whose members wanted to own a business, either for the first time or to add to companies they already had, but that wanted to invest in an already trusted brand. Their desire caused Amanda to ask Mia what it meant to be an entrepreneur versus a business owner. She realized that is what she was slowly becoming, even though that was never one of her original goals when she wanted her own business. It didn't scare her; it seemed like it was the next logical step on the path she was forging.

As she entered the room, several people approached Amanda and introduced themselves to her. She recognized some of them from their responses to her promotion of this speaking opportunity on her social media platforms. They were people who liked her business and her brand and connected with what she might expect from any IT Success franchise owner. As one enthusiastic attendee told her last week, "I planned to attend when I saw you were speaking on franchising your business. I look forward to meeting you and continuing the conversation."

At the podium, Amanda organized her notes and looked to see that the AV tech was ready with the PowerPoint. When he nodded at her, she looked around the room. She saw many people were standing in the back because the place was already full. She had a brief internal thought: "I'm speaking at a standing room only event."

Amanda adjusted the microphone and began, "Thank you for coming, everybody. Let's talk about something every company needs in today's world – Information Technology!" With that, she launched her presentation. She had hoped to get at least two or three people interested in owning an IT Success franchise. She was prepared to take several months to work through the financial details, and then a few more months to provide the support they would need to get up and running, based on what she experienced opening the three newest offices. At the end of the conference, and innumerable advanced discussions with those interested, she had a firm offer for 11 franchises! Amanda was pleasantly surprised that all her preparation was worth the time and energy she invested.

* * *

The last step in establishing "Who" your market is, is to identify where they hang out. Research your market's geographical region, social media, internet sites, publications, magazines, groups, and forums that interest your target market the most. Knowing and understanding your audience's preferences will help you hang out in the same places, learn what they are already responding to, and share content that will speak to them.

We established a solid description of who your market is in Chapter Two; this is the groundwork for determining where they hang out. Most people desire to hang out with like-minded people. They tend to find similar people and communicate with them to learn more, validate their thinking, and to relax in a common and established ground.

The ENO hammock creators hung out at music festivals before they created their first hammock. They saw what was already on the market and realized there was a need for a better product – one that packed efficiently and was lighter weight yet durable with a secure, proven suspension system. Their demographic branding was easy because they reflected their market in need, lifestyle, experiences, age, and personality. As they became more established, they established their headquarters in a location that is the landing place on the East Coast for outdoorsy hipsters. There, they anchor their influencer marketing through their support in protecting public lands, which further connects with their market.

Since many of you do what you already know a lot about, and have been through some type of transformational process, we begin with where you hang out.

ACTIVITY – WHERE DO YOU HANG OUT?

Make a list of where you hang out – what places you go to regularly, what groups you are a member of, what internet and social media sites you frequent, and what networks you find yourself in as a response to what you are doing. For example, if you travel a lot, you are likely to be in many airports. If you like superhero movies, do you attend Comic-Con? If you are a corporate executive, it's likely you play golf and are a member of a country club.

When I first started focusing on my new, targeted niche, I thought I knew who my audience was, what they struggled with, and where they hung out. Mainly, I believed a particular influencer's audience was my audience. I started by commenting on the influencer's posts and resharing his content with my audience. I got very little engagement. Although this influencer became a great connection, the congruence between his audience and what I was about was missing. My assumptions were entirely wrong; they were not my target market – they were his!

I decided to take a different route. I began doing many of the research activities you've already completed from the earlier chapters. I tested my messaging and ideas on some of the Facebook groups I was in. Facebook groups are one of the best testing grounds for confirming or invalidating your assumptions. I conducted several polls and surveys in these groups and determined which ones were the best ones for me to remain a member of, and which ones I should let go. The ones I kept had people that were either great at giving me feedback or were full of my target market.

Additionally, from these groups, I got ideas to create offerings that my audience wanted, and I modified my existing products and services to supply more of what my audience desired. I started using analytical tools and information platforms to gain more data about my tribe.

As my depth of knowledge evolved, and as I narrowed my target market focus, I changed where I hang out. I began writing articles on major media like Forbes and speaking on podcasts about writing books designed to boost your business and increase your influence. The more I narrowed my focus, the larger my audience got. I changed platforms from a little-known one to one that is known worldwide by moving my interview show from BlogTalkRadio to iHeart Radio. Next, I started interviewing other thought leaders and influencers who were making an impact in their industry. My radio show is focused on providing learning and value to help my audience succeed in personal and professional life. I like to explore with my guests their stories of how they obtained such incredible influence, attracting even more of my target market that wanted to move from expert to authority, and then to influencer. We talked about many of the tips and tools in this book, validating what I already knew, and adding to my repertoire, and I learned even more ways to expand my impact.

ACTIVITY – WHERE DO THEY HANG OUT?

Make a list of everywhere your market hangs out. This list consists of your audience, your potential clients or customers, and the people you want to influence. Use the questions that follow to help you cover all your bases. Your list may be quite lengthy. I challenge you to write something down for each item, even if it doesn't seem to pertain to your message, brand, or offering directly. Often, a tiny hidden diamond in the rough will be one of your most successful ideas. Because this list will also include additional data, it might be best to create a spreadsheet, with each "place" they hang out entered in one row across the top. Then in the next row, include examples of advertising or announcements they might see in each of these places.

In the third row, add what they are purchasing while they are there. If you are feeling energized, you can also include additional rows listing how they are investing their time, their money, and their energy, as well. This information will be helpful when you work on building your message.

Asking someone that is in or knows your target audience well to help you with this exercise can bring additional value. The experts will often think of places that are not so obvious but could be quite a lucrative place to know about. If you are a member of groups that contain your target audience, and they already know, like, and trust you, you can ask them what other places they hang out with similar, like-minded people. There is no better place to discover the desires and needs of your audience than to get it from the horse's mouth. Keep up the excellent work gaining in-depth knowledge about your market, because it will all pay off in the end.

- » Where do they physically gather?
- » What trade shows and group meetings do they attend?
- » Where do they go for professional services?
- » Where do they go to have fun locally?
- » Where do they go on vacation?
- » How do they get there?
- » Where do they go to relax or play sports, or cheer for their favorite team (venue or sports bar)?
- » Where do they eat breakfast, lunch, and dinner; where do they get coffee?

> » Where do they shop?
> » Where do they take their children, their parents, or their pets?
> » What groups do they join?
> » What online sites do they hit, including social media, podcasts, radio stations, forums and others?
> » What do they Google in the middle of the night when they can't sleep?
> » What types of problems might they be trying to solve?
> » What is their reading preference, and where do they get their reading materials?
>
> Now challenge yourself to find additional, less obvious places where your audience may be found. For example, CEOs travel a lot, fly a lot, are in airports a lot, and often take a peek at the on flight magazines. Check out the ads – almost all of them target people with money because people with money fly the most.

I often read John Maxwell's "The Daily Reader." I took a break from writing, and I decided to check John's entry for today. I'll share parts of it here because it's entirely relevant to this part of the exercise.

"One of the greatest impediments to meeting new people is routine. We employ the same providers of services. We use the same companies for our businesses. It's easy. But sometimes we need to shake things up and try something new. It's all about getting outside of your comfort zone."

Let's shake things up a bit and stretch our imaginations. Use the following questions to inspire your thought process. Include as many less obvious places as possible – you just might find that perfect diamond in the rough.

» What are a few not so obvious places they might read your ad, or engage in your message?

» Where might they be standing in line or waiting for their spouse?

» Where are your competitors advertising?

» Where are other influencers in your space capturing their market?

» What programs are your people buying?

» What books are they reading?

» What retreats or training courses are they attending?

There are many reasons we want all this information. For example, we want to know everywhere they hang out so you can also show up there. Showing up often, where your audience hangs out, helps create brand recognition. If they see you in multiple places, you establish innate authenticity and move closer to influencer status. They also begin to identify with you as one of them. You are where they are, so you must be as relevant and fresh and as smart as they are.

Now that you know where they hang out and how you might grab their attention while they are there, you might consider creating your place for them to hang out. What might they want that you have to offer, that is different from your competitors? How might your followers connect, in order to feel like part of a secret tribe with membership requirements that uniquely apply to them and others like them?

The early adopters of Apple computers were a quirky bunch, and they loved their exclusive membership that broke from the mold of IBM PCs. They loved being different and advertised it by putting Apple brand stickers on their cars, on their computers, and wherever else they wanted people to know they were a member of the Apple tribe.

One of my mentors wrote a book and carried a few of them everywhere he went. He knew his people traveled in the same circles he did, and he never knew when the opportunity would appear for him to grow his followers. If he finds someone that he wants to meet, he starts a conversation. If something comes up while they are talking that relates to something in his book, he'll offer them a free copy, and reference a specific chapter they might be interested in checking out. Then he signs the book with a special note to them. Talk about building trust and loyalty!

One of my innate personality traits is always to be growing and finding ways to connect. I hope you feel the same because that makes all this influencer stuff much easier.

Next up, we get to the good stuff – How to put this all together and Build your Brand.

PHASE **2**

BUILD IT!

"You'll never know who you are unless you shed who you pretend to be."

– Vironika Tugaleva

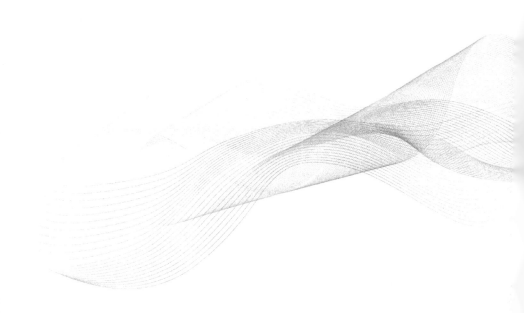

CHAPTER 5

HOW DO YOU DO IT?

IT Success – Your Success Is our Mission. Amanda and Steve sat back at the little conference table in the corner of Amanda's office looking at the new logo and tagline. Looking up at almost the same time and gazing out the window over at their first office, Steve sighed. "Who would have thought three years ago that we'd be here now. I always looked across at this office building and thought about how to contact the businesses residing here to see how they might use the services we could offer them. We could have made them charter partners."

"Why didn't you tell me your idea?" asked Amanda. "That's a good one. I never thought of it."

"I was a techie geek. Now, I'm vice president of your company and training all the new franchise owners how to run their locations and work with new clients. I went from dressing like a college kid to wearing suits every day. All because you came up with the idea of 'IT Success' and started to promote it."

"Are you complaining?"

"No, just commenting," Steve said with a grin. "I work harder than I ever have, but I love what I do. Who knew I could be a teacher and mentor to others?"

Amanda laughed. "Who knew I would be CEO of a company with 98 locations and growing every month. I took a risk when I bought this building three years ago, hoping that our plans for franchising across the entire U.S. would pan out."

Steve said, "You always had great people skills and a vision. You demanded a friendly and knowledgeable staff. That was what impressed me from day one. When you rebranded to IT Success, and we started instilling your philosophy in each office, it took off. Having these logos and mottos that affirm that IT Success will help your company succeed has really boosted this last phase of growth."

Amanda asked, "Are all the new locations buying into the behavior and decorum we expect at every IT Success?"

"They sure are," said Steve, "because it's authentic and feels right giving our customers what they need. One of our original franchise owners say you should write a book on the IT Success philosophy. She thinks other businesses would be more successful if they followed your ideas."

"Funny," said Amanda, "I always thought friendly, good and competent service wasn't rocket science. I learned that from my parents."

"Maybe so, but too many companies that sell services to other businesses forget the personal touch and that their customer is actually a person. I was reminiscing about this the other day when I was on the phone with our cellphone provider trying to straighten out our bill."

"Ouch! Been there, done that," said Amanda. "Did I tell you that that franchising conference I slipped into a year and a half ago contacted me to be one of the keynote speakers at their next one?"

Steve gave her a high five. "People want to hear from you, Amanda. We should celebrate."

"You know we should. Let's go to that Italian place we used to go to because it was all we could afford when we started – I kind of miss their pizza. We always have to remember our roots!"

BUILD PHASE

I begin this chapter with a well-known tenet – "With structure comes freedom!" Because I am a creative person, I often have to remind myself how important it is to put a structure in place when I am building something new. If I trust that I laid the ground with a foundation, I know I can let my artistic side fly. If I forget to include structure, I often end up with an artful mess.

Let's review. We have completed the Design Phase of your branding, and now we are moving into the Build Phase. We will use the foundational blocks from the Design Phase to build your brand, so if you haven't completed all of the Activities in the previous chapters, you might want to go back and finish them. They are essential to the future of your brand as a top influencer.

You should have results for the following Activities:
- » Brand Positioning Statement
- » Values Assessment
- » Value Journey – Childhood, Early Adult, Now
- » SWOT Analysis

- » Passions
- » Market Segmentation
- » Personal Segmentation
- » Brand Longevity
- » Branding Connection
- » What Went Wrong
- » Am I Solving a Problem They Really Care About?
- » How Are You Perceived vs. How You See Yourself.
- » How I Want to be Seen?
- » Positive/Negative Influencers
- » Where do You Hang Out?
- » Where do They Hang Out?
- » Creating Your Persona
- » Creating Your Tagline
- » Create Your Brand Promise
- » Honing Your Message
- » Sound Bite List
- » What are Your Competitors Doing?
- » Choose Your Platform
- » Creating Content
- » Find Your Keywords
- » Know Your Drivers

Now we put all of this considerable research together and create your Authority Positioning Plan, which includes:

1. Personalized, Definitive Marketing Message to create your Standout Brand
2. Powerful Marketing and Sales Platform
3. Influencer Growth Strategy

CRAFTING YOUR PERSONALIZED, DEFINITIVE MARKETING MESSAGE TO CREATE YOUR STANDOUT BRAND

Many high achievers genuinely want to create a ripple effect of influence in the world. However, most of them don't have a message that communicates definitively who they are and what they stand for. The problem is that their unfocused efforts get lost in today's deafening noise of information, and moreover, most people believe their character speaks for itself. Trust me; it doesn't. We must find a way to communicate what makes us unique and then somehow get our prospects to identify with that uniqueness. When you send your message out there, we want them to enthusiastically raise their hand and say, "That's me!" We want them to experience that they've finally found their unique group of like-minded people with the same problem to solve, and they often want to bond with these people like them.

Until I deeply understood the power of Definitive Messaging, I was all over the map. I had several micro-niches, and I had a message for each of my micro-markets. My website appeared to be a buffet menu with confusing messages for each offering. No wonder no one knew who I was, or what I stood for.

We all have many skills and talents we use when working with our clients, and I thought I needed to let the world know about them all. My audience was confused. Am I a mindset guru or a confidence builder? Do I write and publish books, or do I help others to do that? Am I a relationship coach, or do I help executives decide what to do when they retire?

The thing is, I was utterly blind to all this mayhem. I thought the more I showed people what I could do, the more clients I would attract. While I spent all this time, money, and effort in creating a massive laundry list of my areas of expertise, I watched others gain notoriety while their businesses skyrocketed. They were getting magazine spreads, prestigious TV and podcast opportunities, fan love, and most importantly, high-end clients. It was as if they belonged to this exclusive club that no one else knew how to get into. Prospects and partners alike would reach out for them, their products, and their services. Why was I having to chase every client, losing most of them to the same excuses day after day? Some of the reasons were "I don't know where to get started" or "It is too much work" or "I am too busy for this" or "How do I know what you are saying will work?"

I started reflecting on what it was that created these opportunities for the successful business owners around me. It took me a while, but after much keen observation, I finally cracked the code of what they were doing differently. The first thing I became aware of was how they were able to capture a potential prospect's attention and immediately develop trust. The most successful marketers were super clear and succinct in their messaging. I knew who they were, what they were offering, and how they decided to show up.

Then I went to work on my Definitive Message. Working with one of my longtime coaches that knows me better than I know myself sometimes, I began to craft one message! One Definitive Message that wasn't about my training programs, or my best-selling books, or my online TV show topics, but rather an umbrella for all that I am about.

Once I had this crystal-clear message that matched who I am and have always been, things began to fall in place. As I practiced my new message on people in my close circles, I realized this indeed was the deep core of who I am. When I had the "Aha moment," I was kind of astonished that I hadn't seen it before. It was obvious! I changed all of my marketing to communicate this precise message. Also, I began to create a brand – a unique brand that was specifically, only mine.

MAKE YOUR MESSAGE A MOVEMENT

As I was researching and creating my Definitive Message, I was also experimenting with this new technique with my clients. Many of my book-writing clients came to me ready to embark on their next big project, but I realized they had a similar problem to what I had experienced. They weren't speaking from the core of who they are. Before we started writing, we scheduled several one-on-one coaching sessions, where I asked the same questions my coach asked me. Together, we discovered their unique and deeply personal definitive core purpose. Then, with a little creative brainstorming, we turned that purpose into a highly focused, succinct, Definitive Marketing Message. When that message replaces all the other scattered messaging, that's where the brand emerges.

My experience is that working with a good coach that has extensive experience in branding and PR can help you accelerate and nail this part of the process. It's crucial that you get this right because if you don't, it's complicated to go back and revise it after you've built the remainder of your platform. In fact, I urge you to connect with or hire someone that focuses on building influencer brands, because it will accelerate everything you are doing, and it will land your Definitive Message!

I was working with a potential client once who admitted she got it wrong in the beginning. She hadn't put in the work up front to deeply understand her market and what she loves. After already giving her brand several years, plenty of money, and even more energy, she said she had too much invested. She could not bring herself to make any changes. I wished her the best and sincerely hoped things would turn around for her business.

We ran into each other a few years later, and she was struggling – financially and emotionally. She no longer had that joie de vivre that I saw in her when we first met. As we talked over a cup of tea, she said her biggest regret over the past several years was that she didn't stop what she was doing when we last talked and hire me to help her rebrand her business.

I asked her what she planned to do now. She said she was out of money, that she had only a few clients and their contracts were almost over. She was looking for a job and planning to close down her business. It broke my heart to see her like this. As a fellow entrepreneur, this is the last thing we want to see in anyone that is trying to do their life's work.

Over the next hour, we explored a few options for how she could micro-invest in her rebranding, and we started working together in small increments. I am happy to say that she was one of the most diligent clients I've had the fortune to work with. After each small investment, she began taking on a few clients. As her income increased, she reinvested and grew her business to the next level. After working together for the next year, she really skyrocketed. She likes to say that it took hitting rock bottom for the fear to kick her in gear, and she never wanted to be in that place again.

She did put in the work. She embraced the research and deep dive activities to understand clearly all the parts needed to create a more definitive and personalized message. We used this knowledge to recreate her brand. Her new message and brand matched who she is, always was, and moreover, it truly spoke to her target audience.

We tweaked her marketing and sales platform so that she was speaking to a smaller niche or sub-market within her previous market. She only included the marketing delivery strategies that she loved.

Finally, we put a growth plan in place for her to improve her relationship building to increase her visibility and connection with other top influencers in her new market, and she tried it on the world.

Fast forward to today, and I'll dare say she has quite a large following. She is a paid speaker on stages with massive audiences. She has written several #1 best seller books that are specific to her message. She is traveling the world and loving every minute of it, except maybe for the airport delays. I have to say it gives me pure joy to share her story with you.

YOUR PERSONA

The first step in creating your Branding Message is to generate your Persona. Who do you want your market to see, and how do you want them to perceive this Persona? I want to be very clear that we are not creating a fictional character, but instead succinctly pinpointing how you show up, and making sure that matches how your market sees you.

ACTIVITY – CREATING YOUR PERSONA

Review the answers to the activities you've completed. If you haven't already, you should be getting a good feel for your "vibe." I use this word because this is the part of the process where I use my superpower when working with clients one-on-one. It is not a specific algorithm, but rather intuitive sensing of what bubbles up from the research. It's possible that some AI expert could create an algorithm, but as an intuitive coach, it is how I find people's message.

I'll try to provide an initial framework here.

Think about your results from the activities and make a list of words that describe your style, personality, and character. Write as many as you want, for now, choosing those that stand out over all the others. For example, are you or your business innovative? Active? Rugged? Creative? Urbane? I like to feel through this part, but I sometimes use my trusty thesaurus to find more definitive words and to get it right.

Next, I want you to circle the ones that speak to you and see if they nail who you are. Say them out loud. Do they feel like a trusted, worn blanket? They should because it's you to the core. Bounce them off your coach or mirror friend. Do they agree that these words are "uniquely you?"

Now go back through your activity answers again and make sure these words indeed match your research. Are your values there? What about your passions? Do they match your target market's values and passions? Would they want to hang out with you? Would they follow you?

YOUR TAGLINE

If there ever was a part of this process that could use a heavy dose of creativity and intuitiveness, it's this step – creating a compelling tagline. If you are not the creative type, I suggest you find someone who is for this part of the process. If you are, it is helpful still to have someone that knows you deeply to critique your ideas and give you honest feedback. We want to choose a tagline that will be your mantra. One that you completely embody that will speak to your market and have them raising their hand enthusiastically saying, "That's Me!" or "I Want Some of That!" Most of all, we want a tagline that is lasting, and that can carry you through future changes to your market and what you might offer in the future.

Consider these brand taglines that are creative and have exceptional longevity:

» Disney – The happiest place on earth
» Nike – Just Do It
» Capital One – What's in your wallet?
» Kentucky Fried Chicken – Finger-Lickin' Good

Now think about what each tagline means to the brand. If you've ever been to a Disney theme park, you'll remember that every employee, even down to the bus drivers, are trained to create a happy experience for everyone. That's quite the daunting task considering how many exhausted children and parents they process through each element of the park every day. They live and breathe this tagline in their marketing, in their employee training, and every moment of their work at Disney.

What does Nike's tagline mean to you personally? What does it mean for the athletes out there? It's motivating in the least, yes? And it is relevant to any new product or campaign they launch.

I remember the first time I saw a Capital One commercial using the tagline, "What's in your Wallet?" I immediately started envisioning the inventory of what was in my wallet. Now it's a trigger for me in that whenever I hear it, I still see the inside of my wallet in my mind's eye.

Who needs to explain KFC's tagline? No kidding – it's finger licking, although some may argue the "good" part.

Each of these taglines is true to the product or service and embodies the personality of the brand. Now it's your turn…

ACTIVITY – CREATING YOUR TAGLINE

Write five taglines and run them by your creative friend or branding and PR coach. Then try them out on a focus group of people in your market. Pick the one most people like, and that speaks to you and your business.

Once you settle on one tagline, create a quick and simple logo with it. No need to spend time on font and colors, unless you do this very quickly. Use a large font and print several copies. Tape it around your living or workspace for a few days. If you couldn't narrow it down to one tagline, write down the two final options and place them both up around you. Live with them and look at them often. Does it speak to you? Do you LOVE it? If not, back to the drawing board. Do this until you get it right, when you feel it in your heart and your bones. Yep, that's the one!

BRAND PROMISE

Your brand promise may well be the most critical aspect of your brand. It is an extension of your brand positioning that addresses customers' expectations about a product, service, or idea in terms of benefits and experience. Brand positioning cultivates a brand's growth, whereas the brand promise speaks to the value-added and derived emotional benefits of a quality product or service.

For example, Tom's Shoes created a purpose-driven brand story "One for One," which lives up to its promise of donating a new pair of shoes to a child in need each time a customer purchases a pair of shoes. The matching of the shoes makes customers experience the satisfaction of solving a problem and doing good for others.

From the beginning, Google's brand promise has been to be the #1 choice of customers for web information. Do you think they nailed this one? Apple's brand promise is "Think different." Their commitment to creating innovative products that change people's lives have been on point through Apple's existence. What do you think?

ACTIVITY – CREATE YOUR BRAND PROMISE

Fill in the blanks of this sentence for your brand. Make sure you use simple, precise wording with no fancy industry jargon. It must be obvious what you mean to the vast majority of people.

WHAT – The only _____ (ex. For Tesla this would be "The only high-end sports car company..."

CATEGORY – that _____ (that makes electric cars)

WHO(CUSTOMER)–for_____
(for drivers who are environmentally conscious, thrill seeking, early adopters)

IN (MARKET GEOGRAPHY) – in _____
(mostly in the U.S.)

WHEN (UNDERLYING TREND) – in an era of
_____ (in an era of innovation in sustainable energy).

Now write yours all in one sentence, similar to Tesla's:

The only high-end sports car company that makes electric cars for drivers who are environmentally conscious, thrill-seeking, early adopters, in an era of innovation and sustainable energy.

Does it hold true to all your Design Phase research? Does it deliver a unique product, service, or idea to your market that embodies who you are and moreover who they are? Is it simple and clear?

Make sure these are all an easy yes. Your brand promise must be consistent and ubiquitous throughout your entire business or personal body of information. Basically, it is what you do for whom.

THE STANDOUT TEST

Now let's add the bells and whistles that make you unique. The goal is to fascinate and delight your market with repetition and consistency. Some companies have chosen to deliver an extraordinary experience such as Wheels Up, that provides private jet access in as little as 24-hours' notice. Others address customers' pain points like Allstate

Car Insurance's "Mayhem" campaign. Then you have Verizon vs. AT&T who try to differentiate themselves from their top competitors by offering ever-changing, competing price bundles. Others are keen to grab the socially responsible market like Tom's Shoes.

ACTIVITY – HONING YOUR MESSAGE

What emerged in your research during the Design Phase, and especially your USP/VSP, that makes you or your products, services, or ideas stand out? In what ways are you or what you deliver different from others? Does the tradition factor in? Are you edgy or in front of the trend? Is your product the only one that provides a particular aspect of what your customers might experience? What is different from their perspective? How do you make them feel unique?

Review your Tagline and your Brand Promise and tweak them with any new ideas you have that differentiate you from your competitors. After you incorporate your changes, replace the Tagline and Brand Promises you taped up around you with your new messaging. Live with it for a few days and see how it feels. You'll know if you've nailed it!

If you do not experience the connection, it's not right. You can go back and repeat the exercise after you step away from it a bit. If you still feel it's not right, my recommendation would be to find someone to help with this part. It's that important. Get this right before you move on.

ACTIVITY – SOUND BITE LIST

Tagline brainstorming leads to attention grabbing sound bites. Many of the taglines you don't choose can be sound bites you use in your marketing.

» Create a list of the taglines you didn't use.
» Add in any other ideas of short marketing quips that will pique interest in your audience.
» Again, ask a creative person to help if that's not one of your superpowers.

There's also a way to validate these sound bites. Here is what I found in working with top influencers that get this right. They all understood how to identify sound bites that are the right fit, and by that, I mean they are:

» best for your specific market
» best for your individual style
» best to bring out your passion

When I work with my clients, we review their list of sound bites and choose the unique combination that fits their specific market, their personal style, and most importantly, what will wholeheartedly bring out their passion for running their business.

Once we pick our favorites, we string them together in a particular order. This strategy enables you to share with your market fresh, never before seen bites that stand out from the noise, that pique their interest, and have them standing on the rooftop yelling "That's me!," "You totally get me!," and "I want what you are serving up!"

Now that we have your Definitive Marketing Message and your string of Sound Bites to engage your audience fully, let's figure out how to deliver them.

"There are three responses to a piece of design – yes, no, and wow! Wow is the one to aim for."

– Milton Glaser

CHAPTER 6

HOW DO YOU DELIVER IT?

Mia asked the bookstore staff to bring a few more crates of her books out to the signing table. Thanks to proper planning and a decision by an IT Success franchise owner, the giant bookstore in which Amanda was signing her new book was right next to an IT Success office. Any business owners coming for a signed copy of Amanda's new book could go directly next door for a free consultation.

The advertising for the event fell into place quickly, and Amanda was starting to look a bit worn from the signing, handshaking, and selfies. Worn, but still looking radiantly happy. Mia realized that Amanda's upbeat philosophy for IT Success was really showing up throughout each stage of growth. She was a happy person and wanted others to feel that way, whether they were in one of her offices or learning how to run their business in a manner that was pleasant for clients, workers, and partners alike.

Looking down at the book, "The IT Way –Success," with a smile, Mia couldn't get over her client's impact on so many people.

The audience buying the book for Amanda to sign today was varied. There were many professionals and business owners there, as well as people who had heard of Amanda's success and wanted to meet the woman who started it all. The book targeted business leaders and entrepreneurs, but Amanda's appeal and growing reputation as an innovative leader was such that others wanted one too.

Mia knew Amanda's latest phase of growth and widespread appeal came from their new TV campaigns. She already had a nice following in business circles. Her efforts to stay in touch with those who followed her paid off in so many ways. The number of locations continued increasing and had gone international this year. She was in demand as a guest speaker at many business and social affairs. What had cemented her in the eyes of a wider audience were the clever commercials an advertising company came up with starring Amanda. Maybe it was her experience on the speaker's stage, but she proved to be a natural in front of the camera, and the authenticity that anchored her brand shone through. Her commercials for IT Success increased an already loyal clientele and added an entire new level of interest, and not just in the IT world. Business was good.

Finally, two hours later, the bookstore locked its doors. Amanda's eyes met Mia's. "I feel tired," she told her coach. "I thought writing the book was hard. The promotion is even worse."

Mia rolled her eyes in mock amazement. "I know it's hard to be so popular. What a chore!"

Amanda burst out laughing. "Okay, I deserved that. I'm amazed at how many showed up today. I'm glad we are only doing a 10-city book tour."

"You should get home, Amanda. I am not old enough to be your mother, but you have to be on *Good Morning America* tomorrow. I think you have to be there at 5:00 a.m."

"Too bad it isn't *Good Evening America.* The audience will think I look like a raccoon with the bags under my eyes." She stood and stretched. "I am not complaining. I think the book can help so many companies develop an exceptional culture that puts people first. It doesn't cost anything to be fair and treat others with respect. I see that IT Success is in the top 10 of the best places for employees to work."

"Look at you keeping track of the statistics," said Mia. "You have always impressed me, Amanda, but you are excelling at what it takes to grow a business to the extent you do."

"I always believed in having good people around me, even before I expanded beyond my first store. That's why I hired Steve, and then you." She put on her jacket. "I guess I will see you at the studio tomorrow. I am going home to take a nap first since that is about all I will get. Thanks for all you do. See ya in a few hours!"

POWERFUL MARKETING AND SALES PLATFORM

The marketing world is abuzz with the word "platform." Many new business owners and leaders wonder what exactly is a platform? How do I figure out if I need one? If so, how do I get one?

If this is you, no worries. A marketing platform is simply a "stage" that presents your offering to your market. Examples of marketing platforms include podcasts, book writing and publishing, speaking from a stage, blogging, and social media presence.

We've already established that to be well-known, you must have influence. Influence building requires a platform that effectively communicates your leadership, authenticity, credibility, and values to others succinctly and regularly.

Powerful influencers have platforms that they've built and nurtured to attract a large market. It can take years to establish a large following on a platform. When you are first building your audience, you'll want to both piggyback on other active influencers' platforms and begin creating your own.

While this book is about branding, positioning, and influencing, it is not a deep instructional dive in setting up your platform. There are many online programs, in-person courses, and business coaches that can help you learn all about how to set yours up. Once you've settled on the one or two you are going to use, do some research on the top people out there teaching others; then buy their programs and learn how to set your platform up from the best.

The key is to use the information from the Design Activities in this book to feed into creating, building, and delivering using your platform. These are your branding tools. They are unique to you, and they will set you apart from others in your market.

When I first start working with new business owners, I often find their idea of marketing strategy consists of halfheartedly putting into place whatever the next shiny toy is that is trending online. This approach is the equivalent of throwing something at a wall and seeing what sticks. When it doesn't work, they buy the next shiny toy and rinse and repeat. I see numerous people getting lost in the expense of changing things around as they buy different programs, using one brand system for one project, and another system for their next project, and so on. Eventually, these systems become a jumbled mess that confuses your audience, and not surprisingly, results in little to no tangible results.

I know this so-called strategy intimately because I initially branded my business with the "throw it and see what sticks" method. Then, as I worked with my coach, she became frustrated with me because I was spending my energy, effort, time, and money on too many things, and I was not getting any results. I was saying yes to everything and was running after the next shiny thing, over and over again.

As you now know, I narrowed my focus and began using targeted modalities that were unique to my micro-markets, and I also reduced my marketing platforms to those that my target market frequented more often and invested more where I was getting more engagement. As I changed my scattered attention to laser focus on my target audience, the needle finally started to move. Because I consistently shared my message across my specifically targeted platforms, people started identifying with my brand, engaging and connecting. The best thing of all was that people started seeking me out rather than the other way around.

As I was doing my Design Phase research and studying other top influencers, I began taking an inventory of the marketing techniques that I thought stood out. I guessed that they were successful because wildly successful people were using them, so I assumed they didn't need too much testing. I made a list of these techniques and began trying them out on my business endeavors. With my different sub-groups of clients (authors, coaches and consultants, entrepreneurs, and corporate professionals), I finalized what I believed to be the best options for success for each sub-group.

One of the creative ways to find out what your target market wants is to peek in on what your closest competitors are doing. I did this by watching other book writing and publishing coaches and by studying other successful people who are teaching influence.

ACTIVITY – WHAT ARE YOUR COMPETITORS DOING?

Make a list of your top competitors. Google your wheelhouse – what you are offering – and see who else is doing it. Search books on Amazon. You will probably recognize a few people or companies because you likely found your way to what you do by your personal experiences. Add to each entry what platforms they are using. Now add their tagline and a few sound bites they are using. Finally, include what makes them unique.

CHOOSING YOUR PLATFORM TYPE

First, we need to select the type of platform that works best for you. It's essential to choose a platform that you like and that your target market is already engaging in. I'm going to give you a brief introduction to several platforms that top influencers use to get their message to their tribe. Each platform offers a different way to consume information. Know that there are many more options, so choose the one(s) that most resonate with your target market and that you would enjoy using.

Book Writing and Publishing – More than 11,000 business books are written every year and nearly double that for health and wellness books. Writing a book that gets published, and, moreover, makes it as a #1 bestseller, is not always a top money maker. However, it provides much more by giving you instant credibility and introduces your message to your market. You can use your books as what we call a "loss leader," by giving your books away to groups of people you speak to or train. You can also use books to start conversations.

Remember that fellow entrepreneur I mentioned, who carries several of his books everywhere he goes? Recently he saw a top influencer on a flight he was taking, and he offered him one of his books. He tabbed a specific chapter and said he thought it was relevant to what the top influencer was all about, and he signed the book with a personal message. The top influencer asked if the person next to him would mind changing seats and they spent the remainder of the flight getting to know each other. Then the top influencer asked if he would join him to speak on his stage at his next retreat, with over 30,000 people attending. That is how to open a door!

Know that if you are not ready to write a book, many people dip their toe in the water by contributing to an anthology, where each person writes one chapter. You can still be published and receive bestseller status as an author without the commitment to writing an entire book.

Stage Speaking – Speaking from the stage gives you a chance to wow your audience with real-time response that can heighten your influence in a dramatic fashion. There is nothing that beats being there in person to make an impact on someone. There are paid stages, free stages, and sponsored stages. Most speakers begin with sponsoring or speaking for no pay. Once you achieve some success and then create your speaker package to send to booking agents, you can apply to speak-for-pay opportunities. Speaking engagements can pay anywhere from $5,000 to $350,000! Then the stage size, audience size, and potential to influence grows from there.

Podcasting and Radio Shows – Podcasting and radio shows are hot right now. They are reaching audiences that previously didn't participate in this media type. According to Blueberry, there were more than 550,000 podcasts in 2018 with the numbers rising by 2,000 every week. Most people are jumping on this bandwagon because it's easy to set up by yourself, and you can piggyback on other audiences right away.

Blogging – Blogging has been around for over twenty years and hit its peak around five years ago. Today, the estimated number of online blogs is over 500 million. Top bloggers still have a large following, but many of the original bloggers have recently switched to podcasting to reach their audience in a more progressive and interactive way.

Social Media – The latest blockbuster in gaining influencer status is through social media, with Facebook, Twitter, Instagram, WhatsApp, YouTube, Pinterest, and Tumblr as the top platforms in this media genre. If you are in a very specific target market, there are hundreds of other social media platforms to consider. Remember to go where your audience already hangs out. Most top money makers on social media are brand ambassadors that promote their products and services while grabbing large audiences. As of the printing of this book in 2019, Selena Gomez, the most followed person on Instagram, makes $550,000 per post!

Television Media Outlets – The holy grail of media outlets has always been TV. Even with all the alternative channels and ways to access, people who are on TV gain a level of notoriety that beats all other media outlets.

Online Marketing – Online marketing hit its heyday in the past ten years. Many online marketers are still making millions with online marketing funnels. Most top influencers do not use online marketing as their primary platform. Almost all of them have a supporting funnel that allows people to find them through social media or search engines, and then they set up an SEO (Search Engine Optimization) platform that sends people to their website so you can have personal control over precisely what they see and experience.

Leadership – CEOs, leaders, and corporate professionals have built-in platforms in the structure of how companies do business. Every meeting you hold or attend provides a platform opportunity for you to share your message. Even casual conversation in the hallway counts!

ACTIVITY - CHOOSE YOUR PLATFORM

Review your answers of the Market Segmentation and Personal Segmentation Activities, and particularly the overlaps. Now review the Where do They Hang Out Activity results and the What are your Competitors Doing results. See how those answers coordinate with the Segmentation overlaps. Make a short list that combines the platforms your audience already participates in and those you might enjoy creating.

BUILDING YOUR PLATFORM

Once you've chosen your primary platform, it's time to begin building it. If it's a simple platform, as in blogging or setting up a YouTube channel, there are online instructions you can easily find and follow to get started.

If your choice is complicated, it is worth investing in learning from an expert. If I had a chance for a do-over to build my business, I would seek out help from an expert rather than trying to do it all by myself. I invested in instructional programs. Because setting up the backend business is not my wheelhouse, I recommend that you outsource the business setup. That way, you can dedicate your valuable time in creating and delivering your craft.

CONTENT

Content plays an enormous role in the life of today's consumers. Whether people are surfing the net for fun or a specific purpose, if they find you, that is an incredible positioning of your brand. What is your audience Googling? Here are a few common examples:

- » Products and services
- » Personal and professional development
- » Health and wellness
- » Current events and news
- » Expert advice
- » Building teams and engaging employees
- » Growing their business
- » Continuous learning

What does this mean for you as an entrepreneur, small business owner, coach, consultant, organizational leader, or an industry expert? There is a huge demand out there, and it is up to you to supply it!

After you've successfully built your first platform, it's time to start using it. To use it, you need content. Most top influencers write their content, but there are many that use ghostwriters and content copywriters that will create content for you based on an outline or recording you send them.

A word of caution, before we get started on content writing. Your audience has had enough of "how-to" videos, articles, and posts. People don't connect with educational content like they used to. What they crave are honest and genuine connections that give them an emotional response.

Think of the teachers you had growing up. Who were your favorites? Those who delivered the best information, or those who were funny, or was it the storytellers? Although these are all memorable attributes, I am betting you most remember the ones who truly cared about you.

Your content and message have to be part of you. It has to be an extension of who you are and it needs to include all of the Design Phase work we did. If you can't connect with someone, the audience isn't going to listen to you, let alone want what you have to offer. Show your audience that you understand who they are, that you align with their emotions, values, and identities, and that you care. If you truly connect to them, they will be your biggest champions.

We all have a calling to change circumstances for vast numbers of people. Whatever that calling is, your people will not follow you unless you can persuade them to join you. Think about some of the greatest persuaders of our time – Barack Obama, Donald Trump, and Bernie Sanders. Politics aside, each of these people uses their superpower of influencing their followers to rally behind them. Those supporters end up supporting them no matter what the person does. They inspire hope, move them to tears, and compel them to join their journey to bring change.

On the other hand, some politicians don't seem to connect with large numbers of people. They have a strong base, but there's something about how they show up that doesn't connect with a broader audience. Maybe their message is on point, but their delivery is not inspiring. Alternatively, perhaps they look and act the part, show massive enthusiasm, but their message falls flat or is inconsistent.

I love to watch great influencers speak to their base, regardless of how I feel about what they are putting out there. In fact, it's often easier to be objective in my analysis if I don't agree with their message. The emotional disconnect enables you to research such influencers without bias. I watch their body language, their voice tone and inflection, and how it changes depending on what they are saying. I listen to the words they choose and notice the difference in a written speech versus an unprepared one. Watching presidential debates when there are still many candidates in the ring is a great way to see multiple styles. While most of the candidates have at least studied the topics they will face, they are often caught in the moment to answer tough questions. It becomes interesting to see how they handle the stress, similarly and differently from each other. I also make a note of what I think is inspiring the audience, and what seems to be turning them off.

I also love to watch older recordings of famous speeches. They are famous for a reason. I try to find the parts that were most inspiring or persuasive. What about this line or that line made the people cheer loudly? When and how long did they pause between lines? How did their voice sound as the crowd became more and more excited? What are they doing with their hands? How are they using the stage?

Watch a few recorded speeches and debates and take note, literally, of some of the techniques these top influencers employ. Choose which techniques feel in alignment with you and your persona. Start practicing using these techniques in your copy and delivery.

PERSUASION

There are entire shelves in the bookstore dedicated to the art of persuasion. If you haven't studied up on it, now is a good time to do some additional reading. I won't try to "persuade" you to read any particular books because each one out there has a different perspective and was written for a specific audience. Do your research and find a few that speak to what you are doing, and who you are. Any additional knowledge is better than none when trying to understand how to connect deeply with your audience. I would venture to guess that all great influencers have studied persuasion.

I want to make one crucial distinction about my perception of persuasion; persuading is not manipulating. Persuading is compelling someone to do something by appealing to reason or understanding, while manipulating can be unfair and unscrupulous, and is often used to suit one's advantage. Many top influencers are masters of manipulation, and the more you study influence, the easier it becomes to pick it out. That is not what we are building. We are building an ethical brand that you will be proud to represent.

All right, it's time to try it out. Let's create a piece of copy. The instructions for this activity may sound geared for entrepreneurs or marketers but know that this first piece of copy is for anyone who wants to send an initial wave of messaging to their followers. No matter your position or title, your leadership platform is no different from any other when it comes to getting your messaging right.

ACTIVITY – CREATING CONTENT

To create your first piece of content, you need to decide on a topic. What is the number one thing your target market wants to hear about? Make a list of ideas. Also, look at what other influencers are sharing with your market. What is hot right now?

Write down at least five unique ideas to write about. Narrow that list down to three, and then to one. You can do this on your own or bounce the ideas off a few people you know in your market. This use of a focus group of your target audience is helpful throughout the process of building your audience. Who knows better than them what they want to hear?

Some people can sit down and write content without any structure or planning, and it can turn out to be a brilliant piece. While I have a creative side for sure, I've learned that my content makes more sense to my audience if I add structure on the front side. Remember, with structure comes freedom!

Here's a simple process I use to create content. Once you have your idea, do a bit of brainstorming on the topic. No need to be formal; do a stream of consciousness exercise and get out as many sub-ideas as you can and write down whatever pops in your head. Hint – I like to brainstorm with my mirror friends. Somehow two brains more than double the creative insight. Then do some research on these sub-ideas and formulate a simple outline. We are not writing a dissertation here, just a simple framework to put some structure to your idea.

If you are a good writer and are creating written content for your platform, write the copy. If you are creating audio or video for your platform, write the script. Some people write every single word they will say when writing scripts, while others only need a prompt for each sub-idea and supporting info.

If you aren't a great writer or dislike writing, you can record your ideas and get them transcribed. Try the app Otter, which is free and easy to use. Then you can tweak it to make it professional, clean, and ready to publish.

Make sure you introduce the idea clearly, so everyone knows what you are writing about. We often use jargon that we know intimately but our audience may not know. Remember to meet people where they are. Then add in your supporting points with examples, stories, and case studies. Close with a solid ending. I close with a call to action or a series of three questions. Something that requires them to take action after they finish reading, listening, or watching the piece.

Remember to include a soft pitch here or there, embedded in your stories, and supporting points. Be very subtle and not too salesy. You don't want people to experience a sales conversation, but you want them to know what more you have to offer and how it will change their lives. In particular, if you are using statistics or quotes, make sure you write these down during your research to quote accurately. Always make sure you write down the source to give proper credit.

It behooves us all to use a proofreader. Even the best spellers and grammatical aces make mistakes, and it's too easy to lose a potential follower because of a simple spelling error. It is not worth the loss.

If you are using written content, your first piece of content is ready to publish! Upload it on your platform, congratulate yourself, and enjoy the moment!

If you are creating audio or video, record your message. Then edit as needed, upload on your platform, congratulate yourself, and enjoy the moment!

Now go back to the list of ideas you generated and create a second piece of content. The first piece is to get your audience to know you. Then each new piece of content builds on the last one in moving your audience along towards doing what you want them to do. Once they know you, we want them to like you. This process isn't all that hard to do since much of the copy out there is rather mundane. Continue creating pieces of content until you have done so for all five of your ideas. Check to ensure each piece is in tune with your persona.

Before you know it, you've created a body of work that sends your message to your highly specific target market and leads them to the big goal of trusting you. Once your audience gets to know, like, and trust you, you have a loyal following, and you are on your way to establishing influencer status. Give each piece a virtual hug and load them onto your platform every few days. You should begin seeing your audience's reactions quickly. This step is highly rewarding, and you should celebrate its completion. It is the first time your tribe will experience you and your message. Enjoy it, step into it, feel the love.

Now let's break down the responses. Look at which pieces of content and topics get the best engagement. These are topics your

audience is passionate about, and they are foundational topics you can build upon and explore more in-depth.

Internet marketers are experts at comparing content posts. They split test almost every part of an ad to see which parts get a more positive reaction, and they continue using these parts in future announcements. You can do a bit of comparing on your own by measuring positive results. See what works, make a change, see if that works, and make another change. This evaluation is where the fun is in marketing funnels, at least for some people. The key is to analyze the results, assess what they mean, and act upon them by letting go of what doesn't work, and expanding what does.

I want to prepare you for this part of building your influence in that it may appear there are several problems with your messaging. Try to understand that when you are creating such a custom and personal extension of who you are, it's easy to take it personally when you have a less than stellar response. Know that problems are innate in this process, and if you can learn to embrace them as learning events rather than setbacks, you will enjoy this part more.

REPURPOSING CONTENT

Repurposing content is the marketer's best-kept secret. You can write a blog, and then use the copy to create an article to publish, and then use that to create a script for a podcast interview or stage event. It is crucial to keep the information current and relevant. No one trusts an old statistic. One additional note that is more relevant now than ever – if you do repurpose content online, many optimization tools do not like reposting of the same material. You may have to use a different angle. If you are repurposing for live interaction, you are fine to use the same wording, unless you are getting in front of the same audience for a second time, and then you need to change it up.

KEEP THE FIRE BURNING

To sustain your audience engagement, continuously interact with them, and provide attractive experiential offerings that are true to your brand. It might help to create a schedule for creating and delivering marketing material to your audience. Don't let the fire burn out, because the market is fickle. They will find another influencer that keeps them happy consistently. If you need more time to make this happen, perhaps it's time to outsource the task to a social media expert.

One of the most time-tested ways to connect with your audience successfully is to be that industry expert. How are you establishing yourself as that expert? Take your skill sets, build your audience, find that micro market, and keep your brand in front of them.

Just as your house, car, and pet need regular maintenance, so does your brand. Here is a short checklist to use periodically to ensure you are keeping up with what's relevant to your audience:

> » Make sure your message is intact over time. We often change how we communicate based on audience response and create new ways we want to show up. If you drift from your Design Phase work, your message may become confusing. Be patient with yourself as you may have to circle back to ensure your message matches your foundation.
> » Keep your integrity – the essence of who you are – and your deliberate vision at the forefront of all content.
> » Deliver what you promise, and then some. Give five times what you expect to receive. Give back to communities,

charities, and causes that are in alignment with you and your brand. Help others achieve their dreams. Make a difference in any manner that you can, and write about it!

» Watch for shifting winds. Study your competitors, especially if they change dramatically. There may be a change in your market or market space, and how your competitors are reacting is a signal you may need to respond as well.

» Make sure your backend is functioning; the last thing you need is to spend all this effort and energy nurturing a potential customer only to lose them because your shopping cart is nonfunctional.

» Beta test with your lead users and ask for feedback. If they like it, scale to your general audience. Reward your lead users for supporting your business.

» Know top trending keywords for online search optimization. Everyone Googles! Why not be what they find?

» Know the data about your brand's reputation and how others are interpreting your messaging. Use Twitter or Google Alerts, for example. Watch for criticism and address it appropriately.

» Are you enjoying what you do? If not, assess what's not giving you joy and outsource it to free your time up to do the things you love most.

SOCIAL MEDIA

Regardless of how you feel about internet connections and online communication, it's standard in today's society. Communicating via social networks is easier than ever and more frequently used to establish a brand. The effective use of social media is imperative for brand longevity. It is crucial to be wary of what you are posting on social media. Some ways to separate the personal and professional include having both personal and professional social media profiles. Also, privacy settings on your personal page can limit what certain people can see. Having one e-mail address for business and another for individual activities can also help keep you organized (as long as you frequently check both).

First, select the right social media platforms that match where your market hangs out and always post within the integrity of your brand. If you are an executive coach, posting highly charged political information on Facebook is probably not going to help you land work. CEOs are looking to hire someone they trust to ensure confidentiality and unbiased presence.

It's crucial to engage online regularly to maintain the interest of your contacts. The key is to have a clear objective of what you want to achieve and work to accomplish it. Promoting your brand involves an intentional awareness of building on social media and creating content that is consistent with your core values and message. Frequently updating your status, blog, and other relevant sites is necessary. You can also comment on others' blogs or profile information in order to stay visible and engaged regardless whether people comment or not. It is also vital to link with decision makers, connectors, and knowledge hubs. Social media serves as a global marketplace providing you an extensive outreach. Decision makers can work with you, promote you, connect you with the right people for your brand, and knowledge hubs can share the industry trends with you. Once you promote your brand, it is essential to sustain the brand through interaction, learning, and re-strategizing.

KEYWORDS

When people search online for information on a subject, they plug certain words into Google or whatever search engine they use. For example, you want to find an Italian restaurant where you can bring your bottle of wine. You enter "Italian food near me" with "BYOB," and you get a list of places near you that allow BYOB. The same principle applies to people finding where you hang out. Let's say your passion is helping others become great public speakers. Obviously, "public speaking" would be a set of keywords for you. That increases the chance of someone finding you if that is a part of your website, Facebook page, Twitter account, and other platforms.

Google and search engines are continually experimenting with their algorithms of what order to post items with the same keywords. You don't have to go crazy about keywords, but if you are using any form of online marketing, it is essential to include keywords in your online platforms to improve your online visibility. It is the equivalent of a sign hanging outside of a store. They identify who you are and what you do.

ACTIVITY – FIND YOUR KEYWORDS

First, identify your most relevant two to three keywords. Type in your primary keyword in the search box of Google Browser. For example, "leadership" may be one of the keywords for an executive or leadership coach. Review the top 10 results.

The top 10 are the people to notice. Also, pay attention to the paid advertisements. Create a database of the results to be used in your content creation and marketing copy. Similarly, repeat the exercise with other keywords.

TO WRITE A BOOK OR NOT?

There are multiple methods through which you can get the attention you want, but in my several years of experience, authoring a customer-centric book is a memorable differentiator. It is one of the most overlooked and underutilized door-opening tools. It can be a solid growth strategy for anyone looking to up-level their influencer status. Compared to blogs posts and videos, books provide a deeper connection and lasting impact. Digital editions serve the need for being readily available while printed books offer a tangible experience.

The popularity and perceived value of them have made books a favorite of entrepreneurs and industry leaders who want to establish their expertise or dispense information to masses to make an impact.

After I wrote several bestselling leadership and entrepreneurial books, the impact I was making soared. I enjoyed sharing my books with others at speaking events and online. When I started coaching other business owners and leaders to write and publish books for their market, I experienced a huge ripple effect of satisfaction in my work. It is safe to say that books play a highly significant role in content marketing strategy.

Books innately garner attention. They are multi-purpose marketing tools that can be a powerful booster for scaling influence. Here are a few more advantages of writing and publishing a book:

» They are forever. Once a #1 bestseller, always a #1 bestseller
» They generate targeted leads
» They can lead to a passive income stream
» They establish you as an expert and give you instant credibility
» They help build secure connections to engage with your target audience
» They can help you pass your competitors
» They can drive traffic to your business website/blog
» They help grow your email lists

Some people say that "books are the best business cards you can have," but I have a different opinion. Most professionals, corporate or entrepreneurial, have business cards. You can get up to 500 business cards within a range of $10 or $20 online or at a retail store. However, you cannot hop online or go to a retail store and author a book. It might be safer to say that "books are the new college degrees." Forty years ago, only 10% of people pursued a college education. A college degree provided credibility and distinction. Gaining higher education had become more mainstream. As a result, a college degree's value has diminished today in comparison to what it was 40 years ago.

The million-dollar question is what establishes your expertise, what builds your credibility and authority as well as what gives you the distinction in the crowded market.

There are several ways to distinguish yourself. Authoring a quality and strategic book meets the criteria. Your level of expertise and insights on the subject matter will reveal its depth as you write your book. On one hand, the undertaking of book writing showcases your commitment to sharing your message with masses. On the other hand, it highlights your strengths like resilience, tenacity, purpose, passion, and many more.

Brand awareness and attention are essential, but most leaders and business owners do not want knowledge and attention alone. Many want to monetize that awareness and recognition. As we explored earlier, writing a strategic book serves as a multi-purpose marketing tool that can also be a powerful booster for scaling influence. I am going to make this concept even simpler: Books serve two primary purposes. One is to create brand awareness and attention and the second is to inspire and influence the reader. The odds of a satisfied reader spreading a word about your book as well as becoming your customer are high.

Word of mouth may be one of the oldest ways of marketing, but it still retains the power of being better than any other marketing tool. When a satisfied reader shares information about your book with his or her friends, people buy the book because people often follow the advice of someone they trust. Also, people read the book eagerly because humans have a natural tendency to be influenced by someone we know. So, the more people that have your book and recommend it to others, the further your reach goes.

Strategic books use your words to place your story in people's hands while drawing attention to you. When people like your story, they talk about the ideas, philosophy, quotes, and message to other people, and they are repeating what you are saying. I invite you to write a book and let's start scaling your platform! If you find you want to write a book, coaching people to write and publish books is my wheelhouse.

If you'd like support, just email me at <u>contact@divyaparekh.com</u>. My team and I have coached 105 authors to best seller status. Let's make you number 106!

Now that you've created that platform, you are two-thirds finished with the Build Phase. We need to complete it now by scaling your platform as we implement your Deliberate Relationship Building Strategy. This section will share all the tricks of the trade to keep your audience engaged and grow your influence.

"If you want to go quickly, go alone. If you want to go far, go together."

– African Proverb

CHAPTER 7

HOW DO YOU SCALE IT?

Steve came into Amanda's office and placed an envelope on her desk. She held up a hand, indicating that she wanted to finish typing on her laptop. When she finished, she sat back in her chair and rubbed her eyes with the palms of her hand. She asked, "What's that?"

"The latest applications for IT Success franchises, including one in Moscow. Isn't it always cold there?"

"You have to get out more, Steve," Amanda said dryly. "Aren't you going to Europe for a meeting of potential store owners soon?"

"Yes, next month. I have had so many inquiries about opening an office that I delegated the initial responses to my assistant. I will have to carve time out of my packed schedule.

"Same here. I have someone handling our social media presence and website. Since we gained a reputation for being well run, everyone wants to know our secret." Amanda sighed. "I was writing to one of our followers who wanted to know if our concept would work in a sporting goods store. I met him at one of the book signings. I think I have had another dozen people contact me through him."

Steve sat down and put his feet on Amanda's desk. "So, tell me, boss. Did you think IT Success would lead to this? People not only want a piece of the business but also want to copy how we run the company. With your kind permission, I am speaking to a group in England when I do go overseas about how we do things in our franchises and how we carry that philosophy over the entire company. Since you got me started on Twitter, I also get questions from all the Twits."

"The what?" asked Amanda.

"You know, the people who follow me on Twitter. Aren't they called Twits?"

When Amanda finished laughing hysterically, she explained to Steve that they were "followers" and not to call them Twits again, at least in public. Then she said, "I didn't buy into all Mia told me about establishing a following. I barely had time to run our first office. However, I can't believe all the people who watch what we do now. I can't believe all the employees we have. It was all because Mia insisted that I actively engage people on what we do at IT Success. I thought she meant IT and software training, but she wanted us to talk about the business and company culture side of things too. When people ask for our secret, I laugh. To me, it was all common sense and treating others with respect."

Steve got to his feet. "I always thought of myself as a tech expert. Now I am a management expert. If the people only knew that when I check in on a new location, my biggest thrill is checking out all the new software people are using in their business. I won't mention that in Europe," he said with a smile. "I'll get us some new followers, though."

"You do that. As long as we continue to engage with the public and all those who want to know more about us, we'll keep growing. I still remember those days when the only ones thinking about IT in our first office was us! It's still good motivation."

"Yup, and now we have to clone ourselves to keep up with everything," said Steve. "Still, so much better than the alternative. I'm flying out to the Midwest tomorrow to chat with a couple of regional managers. I'll be back on Friday. Are you going home now?"

"No, I have a few more emails from our prime followers I want to answer. See you when you get back!"

INFLUENCER GROWTH STRATEGY

There are three parts to creating your Influencer Growth Strategy, and they are all built on nurturing relationships. The first part is to decide how you will grow your Brand Community or your tribe. The second part is to determine how you will develop your Peer Group Community, and the third is to design how you will be cultivating your Influencer Community. They are all based on establishing and growing strong relationships and thus scaling your influence.

GROW YOUR BRAND COMMUNITY

Your brand community starts as your target market. Then once they engage, even one time, they are potentials to join your brand community or tribe. If they engage a second time, there is some compelling reason they came back to you. They are identifying with your message and starting to want to know more. Those that continue coming back trust you and become your ideal clients. They are the people who most connect with how you are showing up, what you are offering, and how they are experiencing you in a super positive way. They are your true champions and are the people that give you the motivation and energy to continue finding ways to grow. When you are in a groove with your tribe, they are feeding off you, and you are feeding off them. This creative and uplifting space is the environment that breeds brilliance.

Most brand communities go through an awkward phase where all conversations feel somewhat forced. People hesitate to initiate conversations, and no one seems to talk to each other. This initial hiccup will pass if you get them to engage. It is crucial you keep building your community, and then continue to involve them with what you are doing. Everything will eventually begin to flow naturally. It is essential not to get discouraged by the lack of engagement or feedback. If you have clients within your brand community, they are viewing your content and taking it all in. They need some time to come out of their shell. It's vital that you keep offering value to them.

Potential loyal champions can get lost along the way if their engagement is not acknowledged, nurtured, or they are not invited to interact further. Other problems can arise when there is no apparent value to becoming part of the tribe, or the follow-up was annoying or too sales focused. Be on point with potential champions and make sure you don't lose them because they are the most valuable of everyone in your market. All they want is your attention and validation.

There are millions of ways to give your market attention. The best methods depend on your marketing platform. However, in general, you must provide good content regularly, and you must, must, must follow up in a timely fashion. Anyone that engages with you did for a reason, and if you go silent on them for too long, they'll find the next shiny toy that captures their interest.

Your second touch point should typically be more personal, and it helps if it's from a different communication channel than your first point of contact. So, if you posted a Facebook Live video, and people are commenting, you might invite them to "Like your Page" and follow it. Then you can post new cool stuff from your page, and they'll receive their second dose of your message. You can use your FB page to offer a freebie of some sort, to show you are giving without expecting anything in return. Continue providing in this fashion, to help them realize you are committed to their success. By tracking communications and creating a follow-up schedule, you are adding additional structure to your funnels.

One thing I regret from my early marketing days is that I wasn't consistent in collecting contact information. I would attend an event, speak on stage, feel all the love, and when I met with my coach afterward, she would always ask, "What did you do to capture their contact information so you can offer them the next thing?" Ugghh! I left all those people dead in the water with no way to go back and help them.

After a few of these debacles, we began strategizing before I planned to attend an event, or if I was appearing as a guest on a podcast, for example. I always made sure I had a freebie to offer, and people could obtain it by giving their contact information in digital form or hard copy by filling out a postcard. I was finally building my list with people who opted in. These people became "warm traffic." They had some interest in what I am about, and I believed they would likely be interested in engaging further.

One note of reality – there is a point at which it makes sense to abandon lost causes. If a particular funnel or ad isn't getting a good response after multiple follow-ups, it may be time to switch gears and try something else – no need to waste your most valuable asset, your time, on a strategy that's not working.

If your brand community proliferates, make sure you invest in it. Purchase software to support your budding business and hire people to help you out. You are the creator of your brand. You do not have to be a slave to it, especially to the parts of maintaining it that don't bring you joy. Trust me, I learned this the hard way. There are many options for hiring temporary and part-time help, and the options change quickly. Google what type of support you need, and you'll find all the current choices.

GROW YOUR PEER COMMUNITY

Growing your peer community can help you share resources and reach a broader target market. Some people are very interested in sharing with peers while others are not. You have to find the ones that are open to it and develop a relationship with them.

If there is one thing that I appreciate, it is the idea of joint venturing with other entrepreneurs that have the same target market. The idea is that if you promote another entrepreneur's programs/products to your community, they will pay you a nice commission. If you flip it, you can offer your products to their list, and you will sell more, grow your list, and pay a commission to them. I once heard someone say there are so many fish in the sea that we can't possibly give them all that they want, so why not share? This idea matches my values and my perspective of operating from a place of abundance and not scarcity.

Finding peers that have a large following can also help you break into the community. Getting interviewed by other podcasters or guest speaking on another's stage are examples of how you can reach an already interested market.

Leaders in corporate that create a support circle have more success in getting approval of their ideas. It is helpful to connect with others who understand the pressures and demands of working in corporate culture, and having that validation as you move through complex problems helps to boost your confidence as you grow and learn. This synergy leads to more innovation and positivity. One word of caution is to find people who are moving up in their circles. People that already know some of the ropes and who can provide advice will bump you forward as well.

If you can't find a peer community that already exists, create one. By being the founder of such a group, you can create immediate influencer status. Meet for coffee or lunch each week or create a zoom meeting if people are not in your local area. These groups are often no-cost memberships that have a similar focus or goal. They can provide each other with innovation, support, and additional connections. Make sure you check in every few months and ask yourself if the group is moving you forward. If not, find another group; there are plenty of groups out there that are motivated and moving mountains.

GROW YOUR INFLUENCER COMMUNITY

Until six years ago, I undertook to learn everything under the entrepreneurial sun, but I was often going after the next shiny thing. Before I knew it, I'd invested in over $100,000 worth of informational programs. I learned the hard way that I was wasting my time, money, and energy on things that I didn't need.

I also learned that there are numerous outstanding marketers out there selling some not so good products and programs. They were good at getting me to buy, but not the best on delivery and value. Then, there are other new business owners, like me, who have competency, experience, and values, but our message was not clear, and we couldn't get enough traffic to support our businesses.

Before long, I realized that going it alone was not working. Over the years of watching the best influencers in my space, I started developing a few relationships with some of the big movers and shakers. I bought books and programs from Brian Tracy, and I engaged in his platforms. I followed Wayne Dyer and Peter Drucker and became known in their communities as a highly interested and engaged follower.

I'll share an example of how I learned to grow an influencer relationship. Over the years, I had read most of Marshall Goldsmith's books and was always impressed by his depth of understanding. I engaged by providing reviews for the books I read. I realized Marshall was speaking for the annual WBECS Summit (World Business and Executive Coach Summit). When WBECS invited me to join their Facilitation Team and become a WBECS Implementation Mastery (IM) Session Facilitator, I was thrilled to learn that I would be facilitating Marshall's session.

My responsibility was to attend the influencers' sessions and support the attending coaches by taking a deeper dive into the information to lock in the learning.

When I finished writing my next book, I took a leap of faith and asked him if he would provide a review for it. I have to say I was nervous asking such a well-known influencer for his endorsement, but

after a few days, I received his reply that he would be glad to do it! I was ecstatic! Talk about boosting my credibility!

A few months later, I saw a post that he was going to be in New York at the same time I was planning to be there. I wrote to him again and asked if he would be open to a short meeting. He said yes! Not only did I have the pleasure to meet him, but I got to interview him as well. https://thriveglobal.com/stories/leadership-tips-one-on-one-with-marshall-goldsmith/

When I first began working as an entrepreneur, I learned early on that there are ways to pay into top influencers' inner circles. I did this and found massive value for my investment. By being in these top influencer's circles, I met more top influencers, and soon I didn't have to pay to play. I was able to ask for reviews for my books, interviews with them on my iHeartRadio show, and requests for coffee and time together to toss around a few ideas. My status was changing, and I was beginning to be recognized as an influencer as well.

Consider the top influencers in your target market. These are the people you are going to develop relationships with that will support you in many ways to raise your authority positioning. Soon enough, you'll begin to shorten the sales cycle where you're spending all of your time doing what you do best instead of trudging up the marketing mountain to gain a client here and a client there. You'll also be able to increase your professional fees, and you'll have multiple opportunities on the table where you can choose those that make your heart sing.

I do want to warn you that there's a very sensitive nuance to using relationship influence. If you don't get it right, you can ruin your chances of ever being accepted into the influencer fraternity. Once you understand how it works, you can spot it on a dime. You can take full advantage of it in a positive way. However, if you don't know the subtleties of when and how to use it, you can quickly be labeled as a self-promoter and left behind while others continue their move to the top. Please tread carefully. Don't be annoying, and especially don't be a jerk. As the saying goes, "Always be humble and kind."

One of my superpowers has always been relationship building. I'm not sure what makes some people naturally good at it, but I think I learned at an early age to build mutual win-win relationships with my friends because it just seemed right for us all to be happy. Because I was instinctually good at it, I never spent much time figuring out all the nuances. When I worked in the corporate world, I began noticing that some people always seemed to get what they wanted while others remained frustrated at the back of the line. They were struggling to move things forward, to get noticed, and to get what they wanted.

I also realized that despite my innate ability to forge strong relationships, I wasn't always achieving what I desired. As I'm prone to do, I began to study how these successful people seemed to skip over everyone else, quickly influencing others to move their project forward first. They got top decision makers to take notice and then smoothly moved up the ladder.

What I observed was that these people not only had good relationships with their peers, but they strategically built relationships with the exact people that could make a massive difference in their lives. While I spent a fair amount of time building relationships with many people in my professional circles who helped me move things forward on my projects, I wasn't pointedly choosing top influencers to target. I wasn't putting in the time to get to know what made these people tick. I think my hesitancy had something to do with my value system. I felt that if I used influence to get what I wanted, then I was somehow taking away from the other person. However, over the years,

I learned how to hone my influencing skills, so that was no longer true. I realized that if you get this right, you are giving all parties involved what they want. It truly is a win-win situation for all. My journey continued to the world of entrepreneurs, coaches, consultants, authors, and speakers. Well, I made the same mistake again!

I was so busy building a vast network of partners, followers, and clients that I forgot about the value of being selective with whom I spent time with. I was exhausted, overbooked, and overwhelmed. As I began changing and targeting who I spent time with, I started reaping the benefits. I realized that this strategy was probably the most critical business tactic of all. Once I quit hanging out with everyone I liked and focused on spending my precious and valuable time with already successful influencers, my world turned upside down. These leadership icons were terrific! The relationships resulted in flattering book endorsements, TV and radio interviews, speaking engagements, magazine covers, and requests to be featured and interviewed by me on my iHeartRadio show. Soon, these influencer relationships helped establish me as the authority in multiple markets, and when I needed something, they responded full-heartedly.

This kind of influence, my friend, is what I want for you.

Find influencers with your same or similar market that already have a strong following on those platforms and follow them. Provide engagement, feedback, and valuable content to them as they are always looking to fill their schedules. If they are podcasters, contact them to see if they need interviewees. If they are authors, buy and read their books, and follow them on social media. If they offer ways to communicate and give feedback or reviews, let them know what you think.

Many top influencers will respond to people that reach out if they know you are consuming several of their offerings. Make sure you don't expect to do a "one and done" and get a response. The key in this early phase is to get into the conversation by engaging with them in multiple ways. If you begin to develop a relationship with them as the influencer and you as an apprentice, they will see you as someone who cares about what they are putting out there.

Another way to get close to influencers is to volunteer to help staff a retreat or workshop they are giving. Buy, consume and support what they are putting out there and let them know your preferences. You may be surprised but think of ways to support them first and then ask for a favor. It is vital that they view you as a supporter to get on their radar. Once they see you as a giver, you can request a simple favor. As you deepen the relationship, use your prudence to make an ask.

CREATING PARTNERSHIPS

Most people see other people in their space as competitors. I want you to shift your perspective and look at all of them as possible collaborators. Collaboration brings so much more than competition. Competition is focused on the self and is a small-minded way to approach others. People who compete are grinding, and they are more focused on winning than creating real, successful solutions. When you expand to collaboration, you don't have to go it alone. When you combine your unique experiences and skills with someone else's unique experiences and skills, even in the same area, you can exponentially grow the possibilities. When you combine your assets with others' assets, you will probably reach a lot more people.

Who can you partner with that has a similar market, but different skills? Who has assets, resources, or an extensive list that you don't?

How can you help these so-called competitors? What types of collaborations could you develop that would accelerate your goals?

Collaboration breeds transformation. It kindles ideas that might never surface. Intentions and goals become more prominent and more exciting and reachable. There's a sense of responsibility and accountability that happens when you are working with someone else.

Thus, make that list of other top influencers in your space and start engaging with them. The time to start to make more friends is now.

The next phase is perhaps my favorite one to coach. It's less functional work, and more about the heart. Now we will step into our brand and fully live it!

PHASE **3**

LIVE IT!

"I alone cannot change the world, but I can cast a stone across the waters to create many ripples."

– Mother Teresa

CHAPTER 8

HOW DO YOU LIVE IT?

*A*manda said goodbye to the local TV interviewer and hurried out to the stage. When the director of the Woman's Center introduced her, she took a deep breath and walked up to the microphone.

"Ladies and gentlemen, thank you for having me here. As you know, five short years ago I started IT Success in our town. I remember some of you came to me asking for help with your technology at work. Back then, I probably personally came to your place of business to understand how to help you. I can't say I do that much anymore."

The audience chuckled. Encouraged, Amanda continued. "As you know, the world headquarters for IT Success is here in town, and we just broke ground for an adjoining building. As our locations have expanded, one of the consistent needs we have is good people working in our home offices. We are going to need that for our expansion, as well as all the IT Success locations here and in the surrounding towns.

"I have been involved in the Women's Center here for many years. One of the missions of the center has been to help with the vocational needs of young people in the area – both girls and boys. I realize that it isn't only IT Success that needs good people – it is all our businesses. For that reason, I am proud to open the IT Success Vocational Center today. Its goal is to help those in and out of school to hone their talents and passions into a vocation or career they desire. Job training, education counseling, and internships will happen through the center. IT Success will sponsor the center and be heavily involved with its growth. Now, let's take a tour of the facility. As we explore the facility, I invite all of you to think about how you can also help our next generation of workers. After all, it takes a village to raise our community of young people. Thank you all for coming."

LIVE YOUR BRAND PHASE

This third phase of the book is the fun one! It's where you get to be you, and nobody else! Put down the armor, the costumes, and the props. You are going to live your brand authentically, everywhere you show up and everywhere your brand shows up without you.

AN AUTHENTICITY BYTE

Your personal life intersects with your professional life, and your actions from each area of your life need to reflect each other, in full authenticity. There is no such thing as separate personal and work lives. It is vital for both your personal and professional brand to be aligned to establish trust with your audience. It is imperative that you show up authentically at all times because it takes away any risk of reputation damage.

There is nothing private in today's information age. A tweet or a Facebook post generated in a moment of anger or frustration can damage your reputation beyond repair. If you want to rant and rave, do so in the privacy of your bathroom because it hopefully won't be recorded and will not reflect poorly on you. Also, trust no one. I recently read about a well-known person posting something about their struggle with losing weight on what they thought was a private Facebook group. Someone in the group took a screenshot and Tweeted it publicly. It went viral, and now the world knew about this person's innermost emotions concerning her weight, which was not something she wanted to share with the world.

To develop and sustain your brand, you and especially your team have to exhibit professionalism. Everyone should act professionally both in and out of the office. With several generations in the workforce, there are different definitions of professionalism. Define what professional behavior looks like for your team members if you expect your team to be brand representatives through their practice.

TRANSPARENCY

Transparency leads to trust building. Several people assume that you have to share everything about yourself and your business to be transparent. However, that is not the case. In my experience, the best ways to develop deep connection with your audience through transparency are:

» Run a value-driven business

» Share your experiences of being human including successes, mistakes, and learning. For example, I share the story of how my first workshop failed because of weak marketing efforts. Please use prudence as to how much you want to share thought; sometimes a personal story can have entirely too much information.

» Share the latest news about your company, including important business decisions and changes with your employees and clients (for example, when one of my vendor's management changed for the worse, I informed my clients. And, we worked out a win-win solution)

» Share relevant business updates with the audience

» Practice direct and open communication with the audience

When you are sincere with your audience, you build invaluable trust currency.

GIVING

I want to give you a 10-Day Challenge. I want you to find a way to give something every day for ten days, with absolutely no expectations of receiving something in return. Even if someone does offer you something, you cannot take it. Graciously thank them and continue on your way.

Once you start giving freely, a shift occurs within you that allows you to become more compassionate and caring about others. Your desire to gain something begins to fade away. Once you stop focusing and obsessing on everything being reciprocal and transactional, the universe finds ways to give back that are remarkable.

Another thing happens when you make this shift. You begin to see takers for what they are, and you want to exit these people from your life. Imagine how incredible the world would be if everyone made this shift.

When your motivation is to give, you often have insights into improving relationships. Creative ideas will pop into your head to reach out to a specific person. You will become more visionary in how you can help improve others' lives and businesses. As you contribute more, people will trust you and want to follow you. You will become more impactful and inspire others to make an impact themselves. The ripple effect becomes massive.

I often think of The Elders, in this vain. The Elders is an international non-governmental organization of public figures brought together by Nelson Mandela in 2007. They describe themselves as "independent global leaders working together for peace and human rights." They give their time, experience and wisdom freely, and the only expectation they have is to make the world a better place.

GIVING BACK TO YOUR COMMUNITY

When your value of helping others translates into brand marketing, it deposits trust currency in the brand-consumer relationship bank. A few years ago, I had asked my friends to donate on my behalf to a charity of their choice. One of my friends gave me a beautiful Christmas card with a receipt made out to Kiva.org. She wrote a lovely note to me stating that she had donated to Kiva on my behalf because Kiva helps entrepreneurs across the globe. As I researched Kiva, personal stories of entrepreneurs enraptured me. There and then, I decided to donate some of the profits from my book sales to Kiva. As I started helping authors build their platform, they wanted to be part of "Make Your Message A Movement Authors" family where we donated the profits to KIVA. The authors proudly shared how together we had helped over 70 entrepreneurs across the globe.

Thus, giving back not only gives you and your customers fulfillment but it also helps position your brand above others that are less philanthropic. The best part of building a socially responsible brand is that you do not have to invest vast sums of money. Sponsorship can take numerous forms, with some having more of a positive impact than directly donating.

You can also ask your community to participate willingly or by donating a certain percentage of every purchase to the charity you choose. Whenever you are personally contributing to a cause, remember to take pictures which you can later use on your websites and in your blogs to share these moments with your market.

GROW INTERNAL RELATIONSHIPS

When your company's employees work hand in hand for a unified cause, it is going to help them form valuable relationships outside your office walls. These strong internal relationships are good for overall workplace morale as well. Your employees' commitment and thoughts towards your company are going to strengthen when they see their brand doing praiseworthy things for the community.

CONNECT WITH YOUR COMMUNITY

If your company is already an active part of the community, implement a few new ideas to get involved. Attend after-hour get-togethers and local seminars. Join the chamber of commerce. There are potential clients and partners everywhere. Community involvement can help you meet customers outside of your primary professional settings, where you are more relaxed and able to focus on the people you meet.

HOW TO GIVE BACK

Pro-bono Services - Many organizations work with limited funds, such as animal shelters, rehabilitation centers, after-school programs, and community outreach facilities. Such facilities are generally in dire need of repair and equipment upgrades. Your brand can offer the work free of charge in exchange for publicity of your offering.

Matching Gift Programs - Many charities hold fundraising events that solicit donations to support the services they are offering to the community. You can encourage your employees and clients by matching their donations or offer them gifts instead of their contributions. You can pledge a specific amount of donation by your business when your market donates a certain amount of money.

Prize Donations - Contributing to events like a silent auction gets your business name in front of all the potential winners and offers them a chance to experience your company for free. This type of giving, in turn, generates qualified leads through satisfaction and referrals. You can donate gift certificates which highlight the unique services that you are offering, or you can give a highly desired product that relates to the goals of your organization.

WHEN SOMETHING GOES WRONG

Facing Objections

I heard a story on NPR recently about a guy who was playing small because he had a severe fear of objections. He was super innovative and had always wanted to start his company. When he was a kid, one of his teachers had each child come to the front of the room. She asked all the other classmates to share positive things about them, they received a gift from the teacher, and then they were asked to remain at the front of the class. He watched in amazement as each classmate received wonderful accolades about all the things they did well. As each classmate moved to the head of the class, he got more and more nervous, thinking they might run out of time before they called his name. When there were only four or five students left, the positive statements had dwindled. It seemed the kids were running out of good things to say. By the time the teacher called his name last, the teacher had asked him to take his gift, and then they all sat back down.

This seemingly small incident was the beginning of his fear of rejection. One day, he's married and working in a job he hates. His wife asked him for years to start his business, and two weeks before his first baby was born, he pulled the trigger. He was brilliant at building all the parts of the company, but he realized he had such a massive fear of rejection; he could never promote his business to his market. To overcome this paralyzing fear, he decided to create an objection scenario every day for 100 days. Each day he asked someone if he could do something that he knew they would say "no" to.

The first day he asked if he could plant flowers in a neighbor's yard. The neighbor said no and asked why. He was so afraid he turned and ran away. He realized afterward that he didn't stay to explain why, and that running away was part of the problem. Then, he committed to staying in conversation for several minutes after the rejection.

The next day he asked a woman on the train for her seat and was again rejected, but this time he stayed in the conversation. He learned more about the person, and she learned more about him and why he was asking for her seat on the train. He realized he felt more comfortable in direct proportion to the length of the conversations. After about ten days of forcing himself to face rejection but remain in conversation afterwards, he realized it was becoming easier and easier. To his surprise, he began looking forward to the interactions. Interestingly, he found that more and more people did not reject him, even though he tried hard to make sure that the things he offered were more and more ridiculous. It must have been his demeanor at the start of the interaction.

If you have a fear of rejection, I challenge you to try the 100-day Rejection Challenge. I invite you to do it for a few days and see if it turns things around for you too.

Brand Restoration

Sometimes things go wrong. These circumstances might be created by you, by others, or by a sociological or technological environment.

A controversial behavior or a mistake can spread like wildfire, giving you negative attention your brand might not be able to overcome. It's possible you will make a mistake at some point. After all, we are human. It is also probable that you will at some point provide a faulty product or service. Since your brand is in the public eye, public relations problems occur.

If you face the issue with candor and courage even though you could be embarrassed, your brand will stand the test of difficult times.

Your objective is to fix it quickly and regain the trust of your audience. Here are a few tips I've collected over the years:

» Rule #1- never blame your audience. Know that clients can be fickle; they will turn on you if you aren't careful.

» Lean on your support structure – your friends, family, and loyal audience, especially your champions.

» Understand the details of the situation, consult with your trusted advisors, and respond to the situation immediately.

» Take responsibility and disclose as much as is prudent, including how you know if it affected your customers. Apologize to them if needed and communicate the solution. You will show that you are in charge and taking care of the situation, which may possibly create deeper loyalty.

» Share the lesson learned from the pain to help yourself and others learn from your experience. Sharing shows the strength and caring side of your brand.

» Invite your audience to be a part of your journey. Create a strategy to re-earn their trust and support for your brand.

» Get back on the horse and give!

WHEN YOU GET OFF TRACK

We all experience challenges, and you will experience many throughout the process of building your brand. If you know this to be true and accept it, you can prepare for the lows. I like to know what my drivers are to minimize the effect of any lows I may experience later.

ACTIVITY – KNOW YOUR DRIVERS

» Create a list of Distractor Drivers from your experience. These are the top two or three things that make you trip, freeze, move backward, or block you from moving forward.
» Now create a list of your Reset Drivers. What do you know to do that will get you back on track, regain focus, and get over, around, under, or through that barrier?
» Finally, make a list of Accelerator Drivers. These are the consistent top two or three things that jumpstart your productivity and boost that dogged determination.

Awareness of these drivers will allow you to more easily work through any problems that may arise.

Step into your brand with authenticity and transparency, give back more than you expect in return, fix what breaks quickly and with integrity, and put a few drivers in place to help you out when you need it most. Do this, my friend, and they'll be knocking down the doors to be a part of who you are.

The next two chapters are specifically written for two sets of influencers I typically coach, corporate leaders and entrepreneurs. While there are many crossover strategies that work for both groups, there are also a few nuances that apply to each type of influencer, mostly because their audiences are different, but also because they operate in different cultures.

"To impart a moral responsibility to exercise fairness in leadership builds greater leaders of strong character."

– Wayne Chirisa

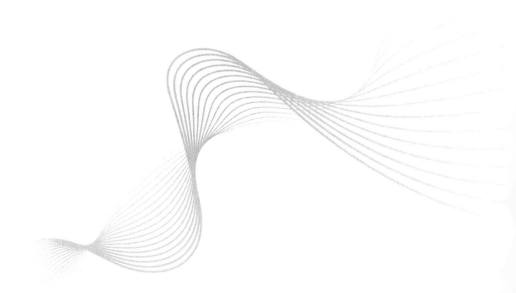

CHAPTER 9

HOW DOES ALL THIS WORK FOR A CORPORATE LEADER?

Cringing a bit, Amanda brought up the YouTube video of her first Ted Talk. She didn't like watching herself, but she knew it was what she had to do if she wanted to improve. She saw herself enter the stage and begin her talk.

"I find it interesting that I am addressing people in the corporate world today. I often think of myself as a small businesswoman, and then I realize that I am now a corporation. Success is due to core values guiding me from the start of my first office. The emphasis has been to provide excellent service with a smile. It has worked well because I and employees, alike, believe in the philosophy of servant leadership. I want to say that it worked perfectly from the beginning, but I went through a great many obstacles before my first office earned a profit. From there, it was some baby steps and some giant before IT Success became a worldwide brand.

"I am sharing mine and others' experiences that proved successful. For things that are not in my wheelhouse, I prefer to learn from others rather than waste valuable time trying to figure it out on my own. I know that what I have done has worked. Being invited to give a Ted Talk validated that. For me to get to this point, it comes down to people. It is working with them, trusting them, communicating with them, and bringing them under your umbrella. When I first started this incredible journey, I underestimated how big the IT Success umbrella was. I thought it could cover a handful of people. Now it looks like the Superdome in New Orleans. I want to share how the lessons I learned in my business will also serve you well in your business endeavors."

CORPORATE BUSINESSES AND PROFESSIONALS

This chapter contains specifically carved out information for corporate professionals. The tips, tools, strategies, and ways to interact with your "market" are not terribly different; you just have to understand your market in a different way. I have a belief that anyone can lead as long as there is someone else in your circle. Corporate employees operate in many circles, and thus have ample opportunity to lead and influence.

We will also touch on how to brand a business vs. personal branding. There are particular nuggets in each section that might spark an idea for your unique situation; all you have to do is apply it to your circles of influence.

PERSONAL BRANDING

I've broken this section up into information specific to CEOs, Leaders, and Professionals. First, I'll share a few insights that apply to corporate employees at all levels.

Personal branding has become quite the rage recently and for a good reason. If you have something important to say and you develop a league of loyal followers, you are in a position of influence. It doesn't matter if you are speaking from the podium to the entire company or trying to convince your peers to adopt a new way to organize supplies more efficiently. Influence is a potent power. It's a softer, more respectful way to lead people, and it does not require you to be in a position of authority.

There is a problem, however, for your audience. People are overwhelmed with persuasive information. It's not easy for them to separate what's important from what is not. If you do an extensive study on branding, you can boil most of it down to wordplay. Some marketing masters are experts at getting the attention of their audience, but they don't always deliver what they promise. Thus, it would be best if you separated yourself from the trickster marketing experts.

While this basic tenet of being truthful is essential with all branding, it is particularly important in corporate environments where even a small detection of disingenuousness can kill your reputation. It takes years to build trust. It is easy to break trust over a matter of a few minutes. Moreover, it takes years for reparation and receiving forgiveness. Sometimes, you can never rebuild trust.

You may challenge me on this but know that I am aware there are people in very high positions that use manipulation, deceit, and shame in their way of managing people. I do not call these people leaders. I carefully reserve the term leader for people who aim to lead with high integrity, positivity, and compassion.

It's up to you how you choose to lead, but if you've made it this far in this book, I assume you aim to be the latter, so we'll stick with that line of reasoning.

In 1997, Tom Peters wrote an excellent article for Fast Company. "The Brand Called You." The book version is The *Brand You 50,* and I highly recommend you read them both. Tom argues that all workers (receptionists to CEOs) must be in control of their career, and it's time we all take a lesson from the big brands. Regardless of age, position, or business, we are all CEOs of our company, the brand Me, Inc. It is our job to be the head marketer for the brand called You. Tom says, "Start right now: as of this moment you're going to think of yourself differently! You are not an 'employee' of General Motors…or a human resource at General Mills (sic)…you don't 'belong to' any company for life, and your chief affiliation isn't to any particular 'function.' Starting today, you are a brand."

Ask the question, what do I want to be known for, and how can I obtain more visibility? If you are a good writer, contribute an opinion piece to your local newspaper or in-house company newsletter. If you are a better talker, volunteer to speak on a panel. Continue volunteering to get your word out, and you'll be asked to do more. Tom knows from experience that "visibility has a way of multiplying; the hardest part is getting started."

With that said, how exactly do you go about creating "You" as the brand? It should be easy at this point; you've already done the Design work on your brand. I'm assuming you've put in the effort to Build your platform, and if all that is in place, you are probably starting to Live your Brand in your everyday endeavors. How can we take it to another level? It depends on the role you are in, and what will be your part in the future.

CEO

As a CEO, you might think that when it comes to branding that your company's marketing strategy should be the focus, but your personal brand is just as vital. Crafting a brand for yourself as the face of your company might arguably be more important than developing your company's brand image. Weber Shandwick's research findings show that an organization's reputation is dependent on its CEO reputation. Also, the CEO's reputation can attribute up to 44% of a company's market value. CEO's stand for a company's vision and it is the people side of the business that people connect to. Many CEOs that have this figured out (think Steve Jobs, Elon Musk, and Jeff Bezos) know that books, media exposure through interviews and articles, and speaking engagements keep them first in the mind of their stakeholders. If you think your market is not ready for a celebrity CEO, you are perfectly poised to take the lead. Do you think Steve Jobs hesitated before he stepped into his authenticity at a fledgling, little known computer company? Would Tesla be the same car brand without Elon Musk?

It's not about you representing what your company offers; it's about being relatable. A Brandfog survey[2] discovered that "when C-suite executives actively engage with their audience on social media, the positive perception of their leadership quality jumped from 45 percent to 75 percent within 12 months."

---

2   http://www.brandfog.com/CEOSocialMediaSurvey/BRANDfog_2014_CEO_Survey.pdf

People have always found allegiance with people they trust, and now, with the popularity of celebrity CEO branding, they follow people they know. We are going to do both!

Branding gives you an edge over competitor CEOs. If your image, personality, and voice are recognizable to your customers and your competitors, you have a distinct competitive advantage in the market.

I'm providing a few tips to get you into the mode of creating more visibility to engage with your audience. You have your messaging and your sound bites ready to go. Use these additional platforms and suggestions to get them out there to more people, and remember, it's about the experience for your audience, and they want to experience You!

Update your "About" page on your company website. Look for inspiration from other celebrity CEOs. There may already be a company in your space with an excellent reputation for culture; check out their CEO's bio on their "About" page. I challenge you to step away from the old, boring convention and test the waters.

Next, update your LinkedIn profile. The bio section should have more information than your website bio to showcase your personality. Create a short, mid-length, and an extended bio to send to anyone introducing you. Include your messaging and sound bites in each as appropriate to length.

Write. It does not matter where it's published, just write. Engage on Twitter, start a "Thoughts of the CEO" column in your company newsletter. Choose a theme that matches all your Design Phase work and provide consistent value. Your audience will begin to associate your brand with your personality and interests and what you are giving. Share your opinion on industry trends and breaking news to show your credibility.

Review your digital footprint. Google your name and look at all your social media profiles. If anything is not in alignment with your new brand, delete it. Know there are reputation management services out there if you need one.

It is also vital to understand that building a brand is not a one-off, overnight process. It is a continuous pursuit that involves consistent efforts of a focused approach, and an in-depth catharsis and assessment of self. If you hand off the responsibility, you will lose preciseness of the brand. I realize you are busy, and the temptation will be to delegate because you probably have people on your marketing staff that would willingly take on your personal branding. Just a word of caution here – make sure you approve anything that goes out, and it aligns with your brand values.

One last piece of advice. While we say keep your brand intact and stick to the Design Phase work you created, things do change. The marketplace changes, technology changes, your business offerings change, as do you. Revisiting the Design Phase every few years is an excellent discipline to make sure you are still on point, and that your message is fresh.

POSITIONAL LEADERS (C-SUITES, VPs, DIRECTORS, MANAGERS, AND SUPERVISORS)

There are many essential points in the CEO section that may be a repeat here, and I include them again in case any readers skip straight to this section because they are in a professional leadership role that is not the chief executive of the company.

While the CEO is often the main face of the company, those in leadership roles are also influential representatives of the company's brand, reputation, and culture. How you lead is essential to your customers, your employees, your CEO, your peers, the stockholders, the board, and any consumers that might not be direct customers (B-to-B scenarios). While you can develop your distinctive brand that matches who you are as a representative of the company, you must ensure it is not out of alignment with the company's brand, or it could harm the reputation of the company.

For example, a very conservative law firm will not look kindly on a young attorney that brands herself as the next Paris Hilton. My word of caution here is always to check to see that your Design Phase work is within the company's culture and brand reputation.

That said, if you manage people, you have an inherent influence on them, and how you choose to show up in your role can have a significant impact on your future. As they say, "Dress for the role you want, not the role you have." Similarly, act as if you have the role you want, not the position you have. Learn more about what the next level position involves, about the business, the finances, the strategies, the reasons why changes happen, the customers, and how the entire industry interconnects. Get curious, ask questions, and be humble in your requests. Know that you may not get all answers in the corporate structure due to confidentiality at certain levels. It's not manipulative; it's how the business has to be sometimes.

Influence and leadership are not interchangeable. People may report to you, which may give you the power to control them, but influence is about creating change and producing results. It's about how you develop your team in character, behaviors, and attitudes. It's about seeing them thrive while delivering the bottom line. Personal branding supports influencing; it attracts success, builds credibility, separates you from the crowd, and brings you and your circle of influence a sense of belonging, pride, and happiness in your work.

Throughout my corporate career, I observed many leaders. Some leaders led with a stick and others led with a carrot. Some used shame and guilt to get people to deliver, and others praised and gently corrected when needed. If you lead with clarity and truly care, you will innately gain influence in return:

» **Give Trust so you can Earn Trust** – Leadership involves guiding people through change and risk, where trust is essential. High conviction brings faster results at a lower cost. Demonstrate competence, and you will gain confidence and loyalty from your team, which in turn delivers excellence.

» **Articulate Expectations** – Leaders that are great at communicating expectations have loyal and high-functioning teams. Leave them in the dark, and they will fill in the blanks, often with thoughts and ideas that are not the truth.

» **Invest Time** – Your primary job is to lead your people, and that takes time. Carve out a significant amount of your time to develop your people. Devote time to create a microculture of success within your sphere of influence.

» **Be their Rock** – Believe in your people. Be flexible and resilient and guide them to do the same. Reward nimbleness, especially if the result is to over deliver.

» **Listen with Purpose** – Make conversations two way. Listen to your team, really listen, especially to those that aren't so comfortable speaking up. Invite them to talk in group settings and ask them particularly what they think. Listen to your peers; what agenda is driving their behaviors? Listen to your internal and external customers; what are they saying behind veiled words?

» **Create Collaboration** – Invite your baby boomers to the table to share their tribal knowledge with millennials and ask your seasoned employees to welcome fresh ideas from the younger generations.

» **Leave your Ego at the Door** – Let it not be a liability on performance. Master a balance between humility, confidence, and fierce resolve.

» **Demonstrate Political Savvy** – Understanding and embracing organizational politics is essential to move teams and initiatives forward successfully. Clarifying what's in it for them and sharing reasons for individual decisions creates buy-in by your team.

» **Leverage Networks** – All great leaders are empowered further by who they connect with. Choose decision makers that are the movers and shakers to build your network.

» **Create Wins for your People** – Think big for your people; invest in their success. Provide circumstances that give your team small but ambitious wins and celebrate publicly. When people master challenges, they admire the leader that asked them to stretch.

» **Lead with Character and Integrity** – Power is the real test of one's character because it brings responsibility. Do what's right however hard it may be. Live it, model it, teach it.

» Throughout your work to lead with an incentive, each of these opportunities provides you with a platform to share your messaging. Return to your Design Phase work often, stay true to who you are, to your brand, and to how you want to show up. My friend's dad used to tell her people may leapfrog you in the corporate world, but if you can look in the mirror every day knowing you stayed true to your principles, you will be successful. He was a smart man; she was pretty darn successful.

CORPORATE PROFESSIONALS

Many corporate workers think that managing your image at work is a no-brainer, but I've found most people do not take this as seriously as they should. How you are perceived and how you choose to leverage your capital are extremely important to your career progression.

Have you ever noticed in your work circles that some people are natural leaders and others are not? I could see it on the playground when I was a tiny girl, and then again in the classroom throughout my education, and especially later in the workplace. What is it that makes others follow one person vs. another? You got it, their ability to influence. I'm not sure to this day if people are born with it or if it's learned, but it's definitely something that shows up early in life, and often carried throughout.

That said, every single person on the planet, except for pure recluses, influences other people. The circle of people that surround you every day is influenced by what you wear, what you say, how you say it, who you hang out with, how you work, and what your opinions are. There are negative influencers and positive ones.

I'll share another personal experience about observing leaders. There was this group of people at work that hung out at the coffee pot every morning. I'm not a coffee drinker, but I would often stop for a moment in hopes of hearing the scuttlebutt of something that might be going on. After some time, I reduced my interactions with this group because they all seemed to be super negative, and it was starting to influence me and my attitude about work. Eventually, one of the ring leaders left the company, and then another negative Nancy moved to a different department. I stopped by again to see what they were chatting about, and the entire atmosphere was different. That negativity was no longer pervasive, and people were working out solutions to the challenges they faced at work. They were sharing personal stories about their families and what they did on vacation, all things you might want to hear from a group of your peers on a mid-morning break.

I want to point out that the two ring leaders were excellent at the technical aspect of their jobs, but their negative influence brought the entire group down. A word to the wise – surround yourself with good people. People that are motivated and positive, people that enjoy their work and find real reward in completing tight milestones. People that lift others rather than tear others down. It will change your world, I promise. If you are the negative influencer, I trust you know it and are ready to change.

Speaking of change, most professionals expect predictable environments, traditional ways of getting things done, growing their career, and living life. That's not how the world works, and I am happy to say that I learned early on that the sooner you embrace that change is inevitable, the better off you will be in your career. If you think about life, it's nothing but constant change. I heard someone once say that people that don't embrace change fear what they might lose from their past rather than have hope for what might be in their future. Resilience to change might be the most critical trait for corporate professional advancement.

I can't say that I was ever resistant to change, but I did learn over the years to expect it, and then to even welcome it. As a scientist, problem-solving is how we do our work. We think we know what might happen; we create a hypothesis, and then we test it. If it turns out, we were wrong, we've learned an incredible new thing that's perhaps even more interesting than if we were right!

I relate my feelings about change to how I feel about problems. They will always be there, so if I expect them, then I'm less surprised when they happen. I don't waste much energy on the front end of the problem, and I can get down to solving it so I can move on to what's next.

This attitude became a magnet for many of my peers. They adopted similar responses to problems and change, and those of us that were OK, and even welcoming of them, seemed to move forward. Those that were stuck in their desire for everything to remain the same stayed where they were or left the company. I invite you to go on a journey of inner exploration of how you see problems and change, especially at work.

Albert Einstein said, "In the middle of difficulty lies opportunity." I offer this perspective to you with a full heart. Make this perspective yours, and you will reap the rewards in spades. Corporate leaders reward resilient employees.

Being upbeat and embracing problems are both game changers in how you show up, and there are endless opportunities for you to display these character traits. What other values stood out in your Design Phase work? How does your message match? Are they consistent, and are they you?

Your platform to share your message is any opportunity you have to interact with others:

» How you treat people in the break room, in the hallways or on the work sports team.

» How you engage with your boss and moreover with your boss' peers, and those higher up.

» What you say, or don't say, in meetings.

» How you work through innovation or problem-solving sessions.

» How you treat the new kid on the block or the woman that's been there forever.

» How you treat internal customers, upstream and downstream of your workflow.

» How you respond to bad news or someone who challenges your ideas.

These are all platforms to pitch your message and showcase your brand.

Ask yourself the questions what you want to be known for and make that happen. Start with your current circle of influence. Your brand is a perception held in other people's minds. Managing this perception effectively and influencing how others perceive you and what they think of you is the goal. The work you did in the Design Phase creates your authentic identity. It is about getting super clear on what you want, giving it all your positive energy, and making your job fun and something you look forward to every day.

"Entrepreneur, with the growth of social media and the global market now local, now is the time to grow your leadership brand."

– Onyi Anyado

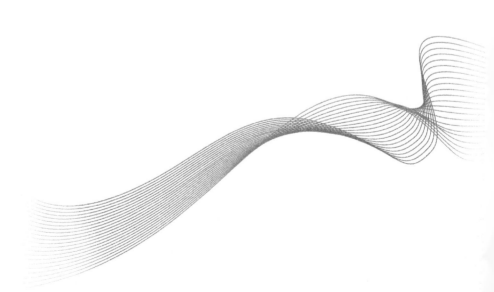

CHAPTER 10

HOW DOES ALL THIS WORK FOR AN ENTREPRENEUR?

*A*s Mia entered Amanda's office, she asked, "How does the CEO of IT Success get to have three weeks off on a boat in the Mediterranean?"

"Because she is the CEO," answered Amanda as she emphatically pressed a key on her laptop. "There, I completed it!" she said with satisfaction.

"What did you finish?" asked Mia.

"A business magazine put me on the cover and wanted me to write an article about what it means to be an entrepreneur today. I enjoyed doing it. I had the chance to reflect on the last five years. You were a big help getting me started on that road, and you have always been there when I had questions."

"It's a two-way street," said Mia. "I learned a lot from you, and I took on some great clients because you mentioned my name. I thought it was great when you opened your second location. Never did I see you creating a corporate empire such as you have. You deserve a vacation."

"Funny," said Amanda, "but it wasn't until I was doing this for a couple of years that I even realized that I was an entrepreneur with what I did. Now we own companies that provide us with software that we use with our clients."

"You go enjoy your time off," said Mia. "I remember being told by someone that I'd rather see a sermon than hear one. I know that whatever you wrote in the article will be a help that any entrepreneur would want to learn. You are the poster girl for how to build businesses. Like everything else you do, I'm sure your article will be a runaway hit!"

ENTREPRENEURS

Many of the strategies, tips, and tools for corporate branding discussed in Chapter 9 also apply to entrepreneurs and entrepreneurial businesses. However, unlike branding for corporate, where business strategies are largely different than personal branding strategies, the lines between entrepreneurial business strategies and personal entrepreneurial branding are rather blurred. That is because many entrepreneurial businesses employ influencer marketing, where either the owner of the business is largely the brand (think Kylie Jenner), or the business uses famous, highly influential people to promote their brands (for example, Michael Jordan for Nike).

What do entrepreneurs and entrepreneurial businesses need most? Brand awareness and attention. The attention is not stemming from an inflated hubris superiority. When I reference attention, it is about the beginning of a prospect's journey with an entrepreneur or CEO or an organization. Without the brand awareness, people do not know about you or your organization or products and services. You need the attention if you are selling products, services, or you. It matters if you are pitching to investment brokers, or looking for additional media coverage, or planning to hire great employees. It all starts by gaining people's attention, and that all starts with creating a great brand.

While I emphasize to anyone reading this book to spend as much time as possible in the Design Phase (you have to get that right first), entrepreneurs should probably spend as much time building their platforms.

BUILDING TRUST ONLINE

Self-declared influencers are everywhere, especially in online markets. Expert online marketers can simply post a question on Facebook, receive enough information from their target market to create a new funnel using proven marketing techniques, and pop in a well-known celebrity or authority to promote for them. They can easily influence people's perceptions, predict their behaviors, and control their purchase decisions by using highly responsive online marketing techniques.

Because of this, the market is skeptical, and as one of those influencers in a sea of others, you now must convince your target market you are trustworthy. You then assure them over and over again that you are different, that you are credible, and that you are sincere, while you compete with people that are already famous.

RELATIONSHIP BUILDING

Although I am a business relationship expert today, I didn't always know how to apply my relationship knowledge to the online marketing side of my business. I researched who knew what they were doing, and I bought a few programs. Then I cobbled together a mix of backend systems and launched my first funnel. Yikes! What a mess it was. I didn't know much about branding, or the emotional side of marketing, and I hardly knew anything about using relationship building to nurture my target audience. Over time, I tweaked my ad copy here and changed out my shopping cart there. Fiddling with how I connected with my audience for a few years, I finally created a successful funnel for my book writing and publishing business and a loyal tribe that follows what I have to say. Today, I've built other platforms that I prefer, such as my IHeartRadio show and speaking from stages.

Regardless of your platform, relationship strategies apply. The intent is to create win-win relationships that help your audience to have something better than they had before. Listening with purpose, making changes to your message, interconnecting with them, and appreciating anything you receive in return strengthens your relationships. This connection inspires them to want more of what you have to offer.

Over the years, I've learned these things about building business relationships:

> » Show your true colors, be authentic, and let them know who you are. You don't have to share everything about your personal life, but let them in on what hobbies you prefer, where you prefer to dine, and where you enjoy going on vacation.

» Get out there so they can experience you personally. Attend workshops and live events in your field, join mastermind groups of like-minded entrepreneurs and forge partnerships and joint business endeavors.

» Use social media to broaden your reach, share appropriate info, and engage with other social media posts where your tribe hangs out.

» Blog, start a podcast or radio show, include Facebook Live in your marketing strategy so that people can experience you in real time.

» Nurture, respond, interact, comment, share, give.

» Most importantly, let them know how to gain access to multiple price points of your offerings.

INFLUENCER MARKETING

Influencer marketing is connecting with the right industry thought leaders and leveraging their support to share your brand message with a broader audience. This targeted marketing connects you with the targeted audience as well as builds trust between you and the audience because the influencer has backed you.

It is an essential part of today's digital marketing mix and should be part of any entrepreneur's marketing platform. Successful branding is all about persuading people to show interest in your brand. The more people see someone they trust talking about your brand, the more they become engaged, and the stronger your brand becomes.

To connect your audience directly with your brand, introduce influencing marketing to your mix. If you think you can leave it as an option, you are leaving numerous people behind.

I'll share a few interesting statistics about influencer marketing:

» Influencer market spending is expected to rise from $2 billion in 2017 to a record $10 billion by 2020.

» In 2017, marketers spent $570M on influencer marketing globally. In 2018, $1.6B went into sponsored posts on Instagram alone.

» Brands are increasing marketing budgets to get the word out. That said, the majority of micro-influencers charge between $250 - $500 for promoting your message as sponsored Instagram posts.

» Trends like GIFs, AR filters, and boomerangs have emerged alongside video content.

To leverage influencer marketing to your brand's maximum advantage, here are a few key takeaways I've learned along the way:

» Choose the right influencer. Not all influencers are suitable for your brand. Tech gurus don't need fashion influencers sending out messages to the wrong audience.

» Provide influencers with messaging and sound bite copy as well as your company identity to ensure they understand your brand completely, and that they are sending out what you want the audience to hear. You want the influencer to use messaging consistent to your brand while giving them the freedom to use their style in delivering the message authentically.

» Employ more than one influencer in your campaign strategy; people in your market will connect with different influencers, and you don't want to leave out warm targets.

» Measure, analyze, and act quickly. If you aren't getting good results, change the strategy to connect with another influencer.

» Choose wisely, do your research. If you connect with an influencer that ends up in the news for something negative, you don't want your market to think you are also involved, or that you condone whatever they did.

INSTAGRAM

People with more than 3,000 followers on social media gain the status of micro-influencers. Marketing campaigns on Instagram exploded in last quarter of 2018. With 80 million photos uploaded daily, Instagram is not only a must in influencer marketing; it is probably the only place to invest your marketing efforts, as long as your target market is there.

These statistics validate that influencer marketing is a vital requisite for entrepreneurial brands, not only to increase sales or to tap into a target market, but also to stay head-to-head with your competitors. Sticking to conventional online marketing vs. successfully leveraging the power of digital influencers could be the death knell of your business.

Additionally, a few more reasons why brands should employ influencer marketing. Influencers:

» Are awareness boosters
» Are trust builders
» Are easy to find and connect with
» Tap into already highly engaged audiences
» Shape perception and impact purchase decisions
» Make campaigns more cost effective
» Are revenue generators

I could write a book about Instagram, but that is for another day. Do your research and build platforms where your people are.

SECURITY

If you have an online presence, you need to give proper attention to internet security. Your customers provide you with information and expect you to keep it confidential, and the onus is on you to make that happen. Use protection providing tools like virus detection, firewalls, and virus removal software. Create secure and reliable passwords that require authentication to keep your login safe. Purchase insurance that covers privacy breaches and includes legal protection in your contract language.

The world of entrepreneurs is a fast-changing space, and much of the information provided in books on internet marketing will be obsolete within a year of printing. However, the principles of branding, messaging and growing your audience don't change much over time – how you deliver it does. [3]

---

3 A reliable, beautiful, authentic brand comes from profoundly knowing who you are, deeply knowing who your ideal client is, having a deep (and iron-clad) understanding of your business, showing up from a place of deep authenticity in your vision, mission statement and your life! Oh, and the most beautiful (and smartest) brands also know their 'brand' isn't static. Let's create your brand story through steps and exercises to discover your WHY, write your personal story, mission statement, your unique programs and offer, client avatar, and how to turn your competitors into your collaborators https://success.divyaparekh.com/yourbrandstory

"It's not what you look at that matters, it's what you see."

– Henry David Thoreau

WHAT'S NEXT

*A*s we discovered during our influence exploration, sometimes we prefer comfort zone. Occasionally, we answer the call of the heart and fire the spark within us to light the world. In this clash, the draw of self-expression for greater good compels us to live each day with courage, resulting in a fresh start every day. That's what our life is all about.

You know, I desired to become an influencer so that I could reflect the core essence of my life's philosophy – to make a massive difference to people's lives. I hope that this book will create a positive impact in your life and set you on the road to your dreams' desires. My sincere desire is for you to become the influencer you desire to be.

You have the strategies and tools in your toolkit to create the quality lifestyle you deserve, financial freedom, and your community to help you help others succeed. When you help others achieve, your success is inevitable. You have the roadmap. Now is the time to roll it out. As you move forward in your journey, let your audience and us know how you are faring. We are with you every step of the way[4].

Committed to your success,
Divya

---

4   If you need help or want clarification on something I wrote about here, please do not hesitate to contact me. Since the first step is sometimes the hardest in a journey, I can at least get you started on the right foot. Nothing gives my heart more joy than watching a person progress up the ladder to the role of influencer. It is my privilege to meet you, and I sincerely hope we can continue the conversation. You can contact me at contact@divyaparekh.com. Please visit www.divyaparekh.com to explore possibilities.

ACKNOWLEDGMENTS

Writing a book is not the solitary experience many people think it is. It is truly an undertaking that reflects the influence and impact I talk about in the book. So many people have influenced my thinking over the years that it is tough to acknowledge everyone. I created a list of people that supported me to write this book. Because I was concerned about missing anyone whose valuable input and assistance led to its creation, I decided to write a note of gratitude. Since I couldn't bear the thought of accidentally doing that, I am sending out a very heartfelt thanks to family, dear friends, partners, clients, and colleagues who were part of the creation process.

I also send out a huge thank you to my long list of advanced readers. It is delightfully humbling to have the help I did. I am forever grateful and appreciative for the time you gave me to review the manuscript and the terrific insights that helped shape the nuances of the story. You all have been in my thoughts during this endeavor. The core essence of my life's philosophy is to make a massive difference in people's lives. I hope that this book will generate a ripple that transforms into a joyous and impactful wave for you!

It is my privilege to meet you, and I sincerely hope we can continue the conversation. You can connect with me at contact@divyaparekh.com

Connect with Divya at:

https://amazon.com/author/divyaparekh
https://www.linkedin.com/in/divyaparekh/
https://twitter.com/coachdivya
https://www.instagram.com/makeyourmessageamovement/
https://www.facebook.com/beyondconfidenceforsuccess/

Ordering Information:

Quantity Sales: Special discounts are available on quantity purchases by corporations, associations, and others. For details, contact the publisher at contact@divyaparekh.com

Printed in the United States of America First Edition

What kind of an
Influencer
are you?

Knowing your influencer type will help you understand your unique values, what are you most drawn to, and where your passions lie. Acting on this knowledge will help you realize more fulfillment in critical areas of your life and become more influential in creating the impact you want to!

https://success.divyaparekh.com/influencer-types

ABOUT DIVYA

Divya Parekh is a seasoned Influence Architect and Business Leadership Advisor who has transformed organizations, leaders, and entrepreneurs across industries. At the core of her work is the passionate belief that connections–both personal and professional–are the cornerstone of any professional's success.

Having coached thousands of people over six continents and supporting over 100 authors, she demonstrates to others how to put theories of achieving goals into practice. Divya has helped professionals launch their careers through the book, podcasting, and media industries by using her philosophy of hearts, hugs, and fostering mutually beneficial relationships in a professional environment. Motivated by mindfulness, she provides her clients with actionable solutions that help them attain six-figure opportunities, media recognition, influential status, and #1 bestselling books.

With over 25 years of experience working in academia, the biopharmaceutical industry, book publishing, and global executive leadership, Divya offers a unique approach to coaching that her clients find refreshing and enthusiastic. She helps leaders of all kinds share their work through a variety of platforms, including books, podcasts, speaking, and more. And her approach works. She has been endorsed by people like Marshall Goldsmith, Brian Tracy, James Malinchak from ABC's *Secret Millionaire*, and more.

Divya's focus is centered on servant leadership, collaboration over competition, building important and long-lasting relationships, being mindful in every aspect of life, and knighting yourself. These methods have helped catapult Divya and her clients to happier, more fulfilled, and more professionally enriching lives.

www.divyaparekh.com
www.divyaparekh.com/speaking

INDEX

Activity – Am I Solving A Problem They
Really Care About? 55
Activity – Branding Connection 46
Activity – Brand Longevity 44
Activity – Choose Your Platform 109
Activity – Create Your Brand Positioning Statement 25
Activity – Create Your Brand Promise 95
Activity – Creating Content 114
Activity – Creating Your Persona 92
Activity – Creating Your Tagline 94
Activity – Find Your Keywords 121
Activity – Honing Your Message 97
Activity – How Are You Perceived vs.
How You See Yourself 61
Activity – How I Want To Be Seen 63
Activity – Know Your Drivers 153
Activity – Market Segmentation 42
Activity – Personal Segmentation 42
Activity – Positive And Negative Influencers 67
Activity – Sound Bite List 98
Activity – Swot Analysis 37
Activity – Value Journey 36
Activity – Values Assessment 34
Activity – What Are You Passionate About? 39
Activity – What Are Your Competitors Doing? 106
Activity – What We Did Wrong 48
Activity – Where Do They Hang Out? 76
Activity – Where Do You Hang Out? 74

Printed in Great Britain
by Amazon

36653140R00128